SECRETS OF THE
TITANIC

The
TRUTH
about the
TRAGEDY

J.I. BAKER AND SAM CHASE

CENTENNIAL BOOKS

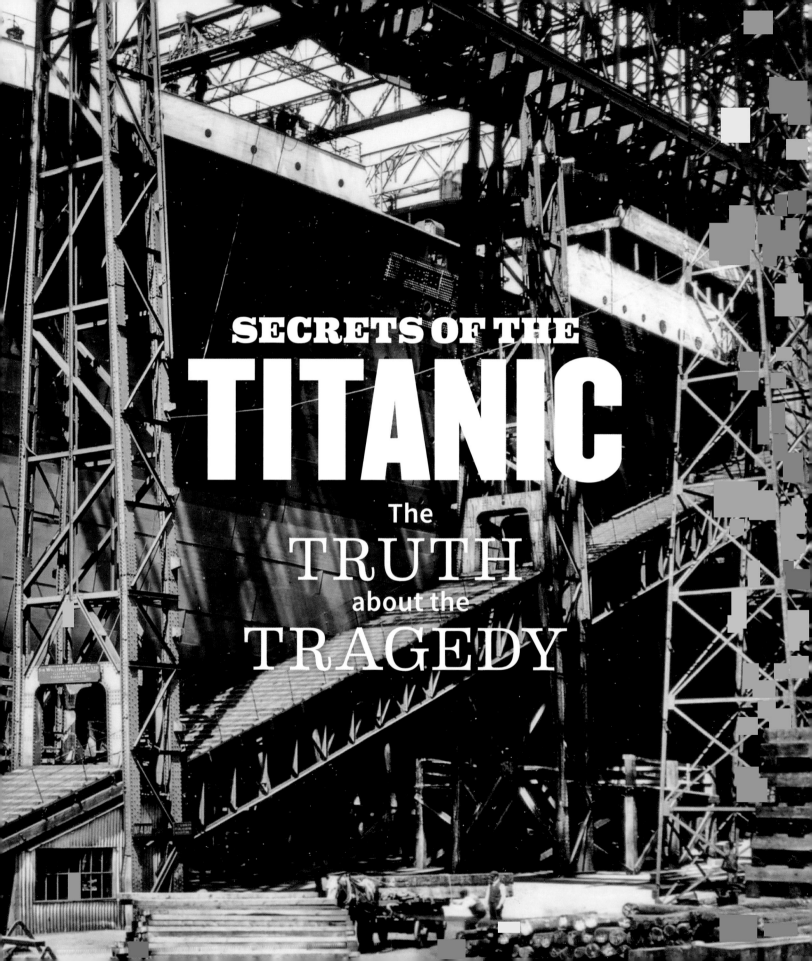

SECRETS OF THE
TITANIC

The TRUTH about the TRAGEDY

CONTENTS

86

CHAPTER 1

The Unsinkable Ship

10

CHAPTER 2

The Fatal Night

50

56

64

148

THE TRUTH ABOUT THE
TITANIC

EVEN A HUNDRED-PLUS YEARS AFTER THE SINKING OF THE LEGENDARY SHIP, IT'S MORE CHALLENGING THAN EVER TO SEPARATE FACT FROM FICTION.

More than a hundred years after the "unsinkable" *Titanic* went down following its collision with an iceberg in the Atlantic, many questions still surround the tragic event. That's partly because the story of the doomed ocean liner has become more a myth than actual history.

When it comes to the events of April 14 and 15, 1912, fact and fiction were hopelessly confused from the very beginning. During the investigations into the disaster that were conducted by the U.S. and Britain, multiple witnesses told wildly different versions of the same story—or told different stories altogether. Some of those involved had trouble remembering the events because of what we now call post-traumatic stress disorder. Others were, frankly, lying to make themselves look better.

The tragedy also created a feeding frenzy among journalists, who were eager to fuel the public's endless appetite for information about the disaster.

One story about the sinking that persists to this day claimed that a black Newfoundland dog named Rigel helped save passengers. Only days after the ship sank, this was reported as fact by *The New York Times*. "For three hours he swam in the icy water where the *Titanic* went down, evidently looking for his master, and was instrumental in guiding the boatload of survivors to the gangway of the *Carpathia*," the paper wrote. It's a fantastic story—but it isn't even remotely true.

That's only the beginning of the tall tales that have spread in the years since the tragedy. It's been said, for instance, that the *Titanic*'s captain was drunk; that the ship was cursed by an ancient Egyptian mummy; that ghosts of the 1,500-plus victims of the wreck still haunt the frigid Atlantic where it went down; that psychics foresaw the sinking…and so on.

But look a little closer, and you'll find some of the most astonishing stories about the *Titanic* can be verified—even if they aren't widely known. For instance: One passenger on the ship, Michel Navratil, had kidnapped his two sons and brought them aboard under fake names. (He was trying to save them from his allegedly adulterous wife. They later became known as "the Titanic Orphans.") Another passenger, Dorothy Gibson, was one of the most famous movie stars of her day. She survived and went on to make the first film about the disaster, wearing a costume that consisted of the very outfit she'd worn in the lifeboat.

This book separates myth from reality while focusing on the human stories that are more surprising than anything made up. Tour the ship's luxurious accommodations, experience its fateful final days, and enter into the glittering lives of such celebrated passengers as John Jacob Astor IV and Benjamin Guggenheim. Learn about many of the unsung souls whose lives were lost—or changed forever—when the great ship went down. In the end, you'll probably agree, the truth is far stranger than the fiction. *

BUILDING THE BOAT

Construction began on March 31, 1909. It took 14,000 workers two years to finish the Titanic.

CHAPTER 1

The Unsinkable Ship

*It was built with luxury and naval efficiency in mind,
but few could predict that a vessel so grand and vast was
still vulnerable to the whims of nature—and man.*

THE
TITANIC'S LAUNCH
*Belfasters were
deeply invested in the
ship as a source of
pride and
employment.*

THE SHIP AND THE ICEBERG

THE ORIGINS OF THE SUPPOSEDLY UNSINKABLE TITANIC AND THE
15,000-YEAR-OLD CHUNK OF GREENLAND ICE THAT DESTROYED IT.

On a warm summer evening in 1907, J. Bruce Ismay, the managing director of the White Star Line, a renowned British shipping company, arrived at Downshire House in London's posh Belgravia district. The mansion belonged to Lord William Pirrie, chairman of the Belfast shipbuilding firm Harland & Wolff. The men were meeting to discuss how White Star could compete with the Cunard Line, a British firm whose newest ships, the *Lusitania* and the *Mauretania*, were expected to soon break transatlantic speed records.

Over dinner, Ismay and Pirrie hatched a plan: Rather than building faster liners, they would build more *luxurious* ones. Their first two vessels would be called the *Olympic* and the *Titanic*, followed by the *Gigantic* (later dubbed the *Britannic*).

Well, that's how the story goes, anyway. As with so much else about the *Titanic*, the facts have become lost in myth and legend. The truth is that no one is sure exactly when—or how—the White Star Line decided to build its grand new ships. The competition, however, was very real. At the end of the 19th century, the Industrial Revolution and the emergence of a global economy had increased the need for transatlantic business trips. At the same time, leisure travel had become more popular among the Victorian era's wealthy, and record numbers of Europe's poor began immigrating to North America.

"NEVER BEFORE HAVE SUCH HUGE VESSELS FLOATED ON THE OCEAN.... ANYONE WHO SUGGESTED VESSELS OF THEIR SIZE WOULD HAVE BEEN LAUGHED TO SCORN."

- *The* Ulster Echo -

MAY 31, 1911

Originally established to build ships for the Australian gold rush, the White Star Line was teetering on the verge of bankruptcy when Thomas Ismay purchased it in 1869. Under his leadership, the firm was soon successfully competing with both the Cunard Line and upstart German shipping companies.

In 1902, the American financier John Pierpont Morgan acquired the White Star Line and folded it into his International Mercantile Marine Company, making Thomas Ismay's son, J. Bruce, its new president.

In 1906, with the help of Morgan's money, Harland & Wolff began modernizing their Belfast shipyards to accommodate the construction of the two new luxury ships. Both vessels were designed by Thomas Andrews, Lord Pirrie's nephew, who planned them to be 882 feet, 9 inches long (nearly 100 feet longer than the *Lusitania* and the *Mauretania*); 92 feet, 6 inches wide; and capable of reaching speeds of 21 knots, or about 24 miles per hour—not as fast as the Cunard liners, but faster than most other seagoing vessels at the time.

Most importantly, the ships would be the last word in seagoing luxury. First-class passengers would enjoy a state-of-the-art gym and Turkish baths; squash racquet courts; a smoking room for the men; a reading and writing room for the women; and lavish dining rooms. Second-class passengers would have amenities almost as grand. Notably, even third-class passengers would be waited on by stewards and served the likes of refrigerated milk and ice cream—delicacies that many of them would never have imagined, much less sampled.

In 1909, the *Olympic* and the *Titanic* began taking shape on side-by-side slipways in the Harland & Wolff yards. About 15,000 employees labored six days a week on the ships—dangerous work that resulted in a number of deaths and 246 recorded injuries, 28 of them "severe," involving limbs severed by machines or crushed by falling steel.

Though the *Olympic* was the first of the vessels to be completed, the *Titanic* wasn't far behind. On May 31, 1911 (two years and two months to the day after its keel was laid), 100,000

⬆ The titans of the *Titanic*, clockwise from top left: Captain Edward Smith; manager J. Bruce Ismay; owner John Pierpont Morgan; and builder Lord William Pirrie.

↕ One of the *Titanic*'s two mammoth 38-ton wing propellers.

excited spectators watched the great ship enter the water for the first time. The *Titanic* was essentially still a hull at that point—it hadn't yet been outfitted with engines or furnishings—but the event was duly celebrated by the press. "Science brings forth fresh marvels with each rising of the sun," the *Ulster Echo* enthused. "Nature has been forced to yield her secrets....

There has been no era like the present one in all history."

This unshakable belief in human progress—so characteristic of the era—was also reflected in the widespread myth that the *Titanic* itself was unsinkable, a statement that originated with an article that was published in *Shipbuilder* magazine that summer. "In the event of

an accident, or at any time when it may be considered advisable, the captain can, by simply moving an electric switch, instantly close the doors throughout, practically making the vessel unsinkable," it read.

That confidence in the *Titanic*'s design was reflected by the fact that its builders had outfitted it with only 16 primary lifeboats and four col-

↑ The *Titanic*'s notorious lifeboats, which could hold only a third of the ship's passengers.

lapsible boats. All told, these boats could hold only 1,178 people on a ship that had been certified to carry 3,547. Though this discrepancy would soon prove deadly, it met the period's guidelines established by the Merchant Shipping Act of 1894, which required all British ships weighing more than 10,000 tons carry 16 lifeboats. Though not yet two decades old, that law had been passed before anyone could have imagined a ship like the *Titanic*, at more than 45,000 tons.

On June 14, 1911, the *Olympic* embarked on its maiden voyage under Captain Edward Smith, who would later take the helm of the *Titanic*. Everything was going well for the White Star Line and Harland & Wolff...until September 20, 1911, when the *Olympic* collided with the HMS *Hawke* off the southern coast of England. Though the *Olympic* survived, it needed repairs that put the *Titanic*'s progress on hold.

Two thousand miles away, meanwhile, the leviathan that would take down the "unsinkable" ship was beginning its own voyage to the sea.

The most famous iceberg in history began about 15,000 years earlier, when snow fell on the Ilulissat ice shelf on the southwestern coast of Greenland. For thousands of years, it was buried by more snow, until it became solid ice about 200 to 230 feet below the glacier's surface. Summer after summer, meltwater dripped into the ice sheet, creating subterranean crevices and passageways. As the Earth's inner heat melted the ice, massive pieces broke from the shelf and moved westward down the Ilulissat drainage basin toward the Atlantic Ocean, about 186 miles away.

The lethal iceberg's journey into the open ocean probably began around 1908, when a period of unseasonably warm weather "weakened the glaciers and made them more likely to calve in the year or two preceding 1912," according to Professor Grant Bigg of the geography department at the University of Sheffield.

Lord William Pirrie and J. Bruce Ismay inspecting the vessel before its launch.

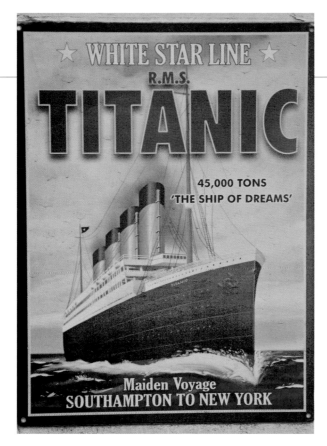

↥ The *Olympic* (right) was initially helmed by Captain Edward Smith and many other crew members who would later serve on the *Titanic*.

In 1911, after breaking from the bedrock, the *Titanic*'s iceberg entered the West Greenland Current, which slowly carried it northward up the continent's coast, from Baffin Bay to Davis Straight—directly away from the North Atlantic shipping lanes. But everything changed early the next year, when the iceberg entered the Labrador Current, which pushed it south along the coast of Canada and into Iceberg Alley, an area between the Flemish Cap and the Grand Banks.

Only the biggest icebergs (about 1%) manage to travel that far south—and even they quickly begin to melt in the warm Gulf Stream waters. Now reportedly up to 100 feet high and 400 feet long—less than a 10th of its original size—the iceberg was heading into the transatlantic shipping lanes just as tickets for the *Titanic*'s maiden voyage were beginning to go on sale.

In the early morning of April 2, 1912, the *Titanic* embarked on its final sea trial—a series of exercises to prove that it was safe—and it passed with flying colors. After the British Board of Trade gave it a 12-month certification, the ship set sail for Southampton, England—its first port of call—at 8 p.m. that night. At midnight on April 4, it arrived and was docked for six days while minor adjustments were made (there were too many screws on the hat hooks, for one thing) and the last of the furnishings were installed. Most of the china, dishes and silverware came on board in Southampton, along with cartloads of flowers (to disguise the smell of new paint).

Much to the disappointment of the White Star Line officials, the *Titanic*'s inaugural outing was only half booked—probably because the British coal-miner strike that had begun in February of that year had made traveling seem risky. Even after the strike ended on April 6, fuel remained scarce.

Rather than delay the launch of their celebrated new ship, Ismay and Pirrie decided to borrow coal from other International Mercantile Marine Company ships that were docked in Southampton. As a result, many of the passengers who had initially booked tickets on these grounded vessels—not to mention their crews—were forced to sail on the *Titanic*. Even so, there would be about only 1,319 passengers and 892 crew members on board.

While the *Titanic*'s passenger list may have lacked volume, it more than made up for that in high-society glamour. Nicknamed the "Millionaire's Special," the ship attracted a virtual who's who of the period's rich and famous. Among the notables on board were Benjamin Guggenheim, who was traveling with his mistress; Macy's co-owner Isidor Straus and his wife, Ida; and the movie star Dorothy Gibson. The ship's richest passenger was John Jacob Astor IV, who was 47 and sailing with his pregnant 18-year-old wife. They had all paid a steep price for their luxurious accommodations: A first-class cabin on the *Titanic* cost at least $600, about $13,000 in today's dollars—which, at the time, was more than twice what American laborers or schoolteachers earned in an entire year. (It wasn't only for the upper crust, however; third-class accommodations could be purchased for as little as $26.50.)

J. Bruce Ismay himself was so impressed by the guests on the maiden voyage that he decided to join them—as did ship designer Thomas Andrews. Though Lord Pirrie had planned to go as well, poor health forced him to cancel at the last minute, while John Pierpont Morgan bowed out because of business commitments. (That's what he said—though in truth, he may have been enjoying the spas in Aix-les-Bains, France.)

At 11:45 a.m. on April 10, 1912, crowds packed the Southampton docks as the *Titanic*'s bells clanged, hatchways were closed and the crew cried "All ashore!" By noon, the ship was pulling away from its moorings.

"The great vessel moved in slow majesty down Southampton water," spectator Ernest Townley had said.

THE ONLY KNOWN PHOTO
...of the Titanic's berg shows a stripe that allegedly came from the ship's hull.

New Quadruple Turbine
The Largest Vessel Afloat.

Lusitania.

32,500 tons. 68,000 horse power
Length 785 ft. Breadth 83 ft. Depth 60 ft. 6 in

S.S. LUSITANIA

The dimensions of the
Q. T. S. S. *Mauretania* are:
Length Overall • • 787 ft
Between Perpendicu-
lars, • • • 760 ft
Beam, • • • 88 ft.
Depth, • • 60 ft. 6 in.
Gross Tonnage, • 33,200.
Maximum Draught, 37 ft.
corresponding to a Dis-
placement of 43,000 tons.
The I. H. P. of her Turbines
being 68,000, she can travel
27 knots per hour.

(QUADRUPLE TURBINE) S.S. MAURETANIA.
THE LARGEST VESSEL AFLOAT.

"IT WAS THE DEPARTURE OF A WONDER SHIP— A FLOATING PALACE THAT FAR EXCELLED ALL OTHERS IN SIZE AND MAGNIFICENCE, AND MEN SAID SHE COULD NOT SINK."

- Roberta Maioni -

MAID TO THE COUNTESS OF ROTHES,
A FIRST-CLASS PASSENGER

⬆ The *Titanic* was built partly to compete with the *Lusitania* (top of page) and *Mauretania* (above), the world's first superliners and the largest ships ever built up to that time.

"Passengers waved farewells from her decks and windows and a mob of jolly stokers yelled from the forecastle side."

But the celebratory mood was interrupted when suction from the ship's massive hull snapped the hawsers of the nearby SS *New York* ("like the crack of a gun," according to one account), sending the smaller liner hurling toward the *Titanic*. At the last minute, the collision was narrowly averted by the intervention of two tugboats.

"It was a relief to everyone when the *Titanic* at last passed the bend and glided slowly away to sea," the *Birmingham Daily Gazette* reported the next day. "It was a thrilling start for the maiden voyage of the largest steamer in the world."

The *Titanic* was now heading across the English Channel to Cherbourg, France, where it arrived at 6:35 p.m. After picking up about 280 additional passengers—mostly wealthy Americans and poor Irish immigrants—it continued on to Queenstown, Ireland, where it arrived around noon on April 11, dropping off seven lucky souls and picking up 123 unlucky new ones. It was the ship's last port of call. At 1:30 p.m., the *Titanic* sailed into the Atlantic on a collision course with an iceberg that had been 15,000 years in the making. ✳

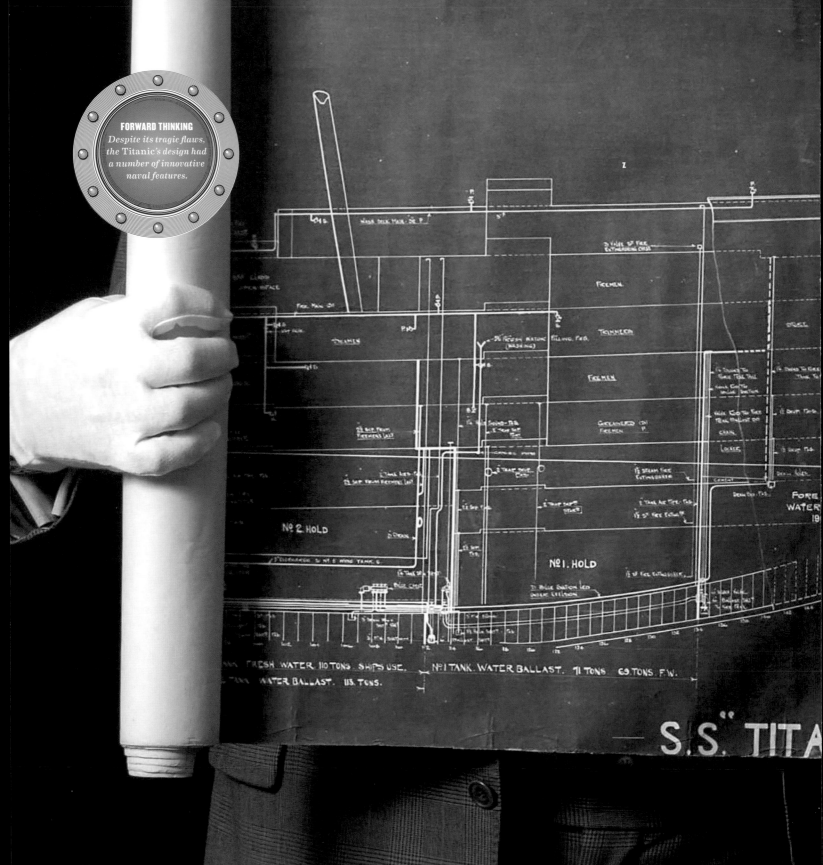

FRESH WATER 110 TONS SHIPS USE.   N°1 TANK. WATER BALLAST.   71 TONS   69 TONS F.W.

WATER BALLAST.   113 TONS.

S.S. "TITA

THE *TITANIC* FROM BOW TO STERN

*FROM FIRST-CLASS RESTAURANTS TO THE BOILER ROOMS,
TAKE A TOUR OF SOME OF THE MOST NOTEWORTHY
AREAS ON THE WORLD'S MOST FAMOUS VESSEL.*

1 | POOP DECK Originally designed to help ships avoid being swamped by waves at the rear, poop decks had mostly outlasted their usefulness by the time the *Titanic* set sail—in fact, the ship was one of the last major passenger liners to feature one. The deck was mostly used as a promenade for third-class passengers.

2 | THIRD-CLASS GENERAL ROOM The social hub for steerage passengers, this room contained a piano, tables and benches. A party was held here on the night the ship sank. Lights were turned off at 10.

3 | THIRD-CLASS CABINS Not surprisingly, these were located in the most undesirable part of the ship, where passengers were often disturbed by the sound of the engines and the motion of the vessel. This was the first area to flood after the ship hit the iceberg.

4 | AFT WELL DECK This area was one of two well decks on the ship. (See 21.) They were connected by an area known as Scotland Road, which was used by crew members to easily travel from one side of the ship to the other. Many of the crew members were Liverpudlians, who named the passageway after a major road in the northern reaches of their city. On this deck (and the poop deck), the last of the passengers desperately clung on for their lives just before the ship plunged into the ocean.

5 | SECOND-CLASS CABINS This is where second-class passengers slept. To the fore of the cabin area was the second-class dining saloon. Just in front of that was the ship's hospital ward.

6 | SECOND-CLASS PROMENADE Located above the second-class dining saloon, this was one of three second-class promenade areas on the *Titanic* and the only one that was enclosed. As such, it was largely used as a play area for children.

7 | TURBINE ENGINE ROOM Along with the reciprocating engine room (fore of the turbine), this was the source of the ship's horsepower.

8 | SECOND-CLASS ENTRANCE This was located on the boat deck, where the lifeboats were stored. It was the last of the decks to flood—at around 2:05 a.m.—during the ship's tragic final moments.

9 | VERANDAH CAFÉ There were two Verandah Cafés on the *Titanic*. This one, on the starboard side, was for nonsmokers. The first-class smoking room was fore of the café, while the À la Carte Restaurant was just beneath it.

10 | FOURTH FUNNEL Unlike the ship's three other funnels, this one didn't serve as an outlet for smoke from the ship's boilers—it was added to make the ship look more elegant and powerful, although it may also have been used for general ventilation purposes.

11 | AFT GRAND STAIRCASE The second of the ship's two grand staircases, this led down to the Café Parisien. The more elaborate and striking grand staircase toward the front of the ship is the one featured in the James Cameron film.

12 | FIRST-CLASS PROMENADE This thoroughfare for the ship's wealthiest passengers extended nearly 500 feet across the length of the liner.

13 | FIRST-CLASS SOCIAL AREAS Many of the ship's most lavish features were located on the decks below the second and third funnels— partly because this was the quietest, smoothest-sailing part of the liner. They included the first-class lounge, first-class staterooms and the first-class dining saloon.

14 | ADDITIONAL FIRST-CLASS SOCIAL AREAS The decks below the second funnel included the gymnasium, a private promenade, the first-class reception room and the entrance to the first-class dining room. The Turkish baths were below the reception room and the squash racquet court was just fore of the baths.

15 | ONE OF SIX BOILER ROOMS There were 29 coal-fired boilers on the *Titanic*, all manned by the so-called "Black Gang," a group of stokers who fueled the machinery 24 hours a day.

16 | FORE GRAND STAIRCASE Arguably the most magnificent staircase ever installed on a ship—before or since—this was the aesthetic centerpiece of the *Titanic*'s first-class accommodations and became one of the most striking backdrops in Cameron's *Titanic*. On D Deck, the staircase accessed the reception room and first-class dining saloon.

17 | OFFICERS' QUARTERS These consisted of the captain's room, the wheelhouse, the officers' smoking room, the pilot room, the navigating room and the chart room.

18 | FIRST FUNNEL This funnel was probably the second to collapse (after the second funnel) during the sinking—possibly because a coal explosion or the impact of one of the emergency flares caused the ship to roll, which compromised the funnel.

19 | BRIDGE AND WHEELHOUSE Before the widespread use of modern technology, the best way for a captain to evaluate the conditions on an ocean voyage was just to look—and that's primarily what the ship's bridge was for. The wheelhouse, where the ship was steered, was inside the bridge structure.

20 | FIRST-CLASS BAGGAGE, POST OFFICE AND MAILROOM These adjacent areas were among the first to flood after the collision. Until the very end, *Titanic* crew members were seen trying to save registered mail from water damage, because they believed the ship wouldn't sink for at least eight hours (it would last less than three).

21 | FORECASTLE WELL DECK Located on C Deck, this was one of two well decks on the *Titanic*. (See 4.)

22 | CARGO HOLD Among the items stored in the *Titanic*: eight cases of orchids, one case of Edison gramophones, 75 bales of fish, 11 bales of rubber, 76 cases of something called "dragon's blood," 79 goat skins and 12 cases of ostrich feathers.

23 | THE CROW'S NEST This is where lookout Frederick Fleet rang the bell three times to signal the deck that he had seen the iceberg. It came, he later said, out of a haze.

24 | DAMAGED COMPARTMENTS The lower part of the *Titanic* consisted of 16 watertight compartments. The collision with the iceberg tore open the hull, compromising the six of them in this area. Although the doors were closed soon after the collision, the weight of the water in the compromised compartments caused the ship to lean forward. Unfortunately, the compartments were watertight only horizontally, as their tops had been left open. Thus, when the ship tilted, water flowed over them into the rest of the ship, causing it to founder.

25 | FORECASTLE DECK The 106-foot-long deck remains relatively intact even today as it lies on the bottom of the Atlantic and is one of the most photographed parts of the legendary wreck.

26 | ANCHOR CRANE When the first images of the *Titanic* wreck became public, some were struck by the fact that the undamaged anchor crane —usually facing aft—was turned 180 degrees directly forward. To this day, no one is quite sure why. *

LIFELONG SEAFARER
Captain Smith quit school at age 12. He joined his first crew as a teen and worked his way up through the ranks.

THE CREW'S LIVES AND LOSS

OF THE 1,500-PLUS FATALITIES, ABOUT 688 STAFFERS—FROM STEWARDS TO OFFICERS—WENT DOWN WITH THE SHIP.

THE OFFICERS

CAPTAIN
Commander Edward Smith
Perished

Known as "The Millionaires' Captain," Smith began working for the White Star Line in 1880, and started helming White Star Line's newest flagship vessels a few years later. At age 62 and with 27 years of experience at command under his belt, Smith was one of the world's most seasoned ship captains when he stepped aboard the *Titanic* in 1912. He went down with his ship, with some accounts claiming that he urged his crew to "be British" in his final words. The phrase is engraved on his memorial in Staffordshire, the English county in which he was born.

CHIEF OFFICER
Henry Tingle Wilde
Perished

Wilde had prior experience as second-in-command to Edward Smith prior to their time on the *Titanic*, having served under Smith on the *Olympic*. He also worked on 10 White Star Line ships before *Titanic*. Sadly, Wilde was no stranger to tragedy before the ill-fated voyage: His wife and twin sons had passed away in December 1910, possibly from scarlet fever. Like many who died in the wreck, there are conflicting reports of where Wilde was last seen before the ship went down. A separate rumor suggests Wilde wrote a letter to his sister while on board, saying that he had "a queer feeling about the ship."

FIRST OFFICER
William McMaster Murdoch
Perished

It was Murdoch who was in command in the late-night hours of April 14 when the infamous iceberg came into view. He gave orders to turn the ship, but it was already too late. Once it became clear that the *Titanic* was going down, Murdoch led the starboard evacuation, ushering passengers into lifeboats and tossing deck chairs for those in the water to use as flotation devices. After the 1997 *Titanic* film depicted Murdoch killing a passenger and then himself, a 20th Century Fox executive flew to Scotland to apologize to Murdoch's elderly nephew for the negative portrayal.

SECOND OFFICER
Charles Lightoller
Collapsible Lifeboat B

Lightoller is perhaps best remembered in the *Titanic* disaster for strictly enforcing a women-and-children-only policy that ensured vulnerable lives were saved, but also sent several lifeboats away with unfilled capacities. He himself escaped aboard a lifeboat, although only after diving into the water and nearly drowning alongside the ship's wreckage. He would later serve as a commanding officer in the Royal Navy during World War I. Post-retirement, he was also a hero in World War II, saving 127 British soldiers in his personal boat during the evacuation of Dunkirk, France.

THIRD OFFICER

Herbert Pitman

Lifeboat 5

When Pitman was instructed by First Officer William Murdoch to take charge on Lifeboat 5, he thought it was a precautionary measure. He soon learned that wasn't the case. As instructed, Pitman directed the lifeboat to the ship's gangway doors to collect more evacuees, but the doors never opened. When he later suggested turning the lifeboat around to save those flailing in the water, the passengers in the half-full boat refused, claiming they'd be pulled underwater themselves by the drowning people competing for space. After the disaster, Pitman continued working on ships for White Star Line.

FOURTH OFFICER

Joseph Boxhall

Lifeboat 2

Just before his lifeboat lowered into the water, Boxhall grabbed a box of green lights to use as a signal, and he did everything he could to attract the attention of rescuers as the *Titanic* sank. At first, his efforts were in vain: The Morse code lamp signals and distress flares he sent up went unanswered by the nearby SS *Californian*. Hours later, however, he succeeded in getting the attention of the *Carpathia* by sending up green flares, helping save many lives, including his own. He'd continue to serve for White Star Line for nearly 30 years after the accident. Boxhall died in 1967 at age 83, the last surviving officer of the *Titanic*.

FIFTH OFFICER

Harold Lowe

Lifeboat 14

Lowe was 29 years old in 1912, but already had plenty of seafaring experience after running away from home and joining the Merchant Navy at the age of 14. Based on the events of the *Titanic*'s sinking, Lowe hadn't lost much edge since his teenage years. When hassled by White Star Line chairman J. Bruce Ismay to lower lifeboats into the water more quickly, Lowe replied to the company chief, "If you will get to hell out of [the way] I shall be able to do something." Later, during the American inquiry into the disaster, he was asked what an iceberg was made of. "Ice, I suppose, sir," Lowe responded.

SIXTH OFFICER

James Moody

Perished

After loading up several of the lifeboats with women and children, Lifeboat 14 represented Moody's chance at survival—his spot in the officer pecking order would have dictated that he enter the raft to help guide its occupants to safety. Instead, the 24-year-old Moody surrendered the spot to Fifth Officer Harold Lowe, a move that he knew would surely lead to his own death. A monument in Moody's hometown of Scarborough, England, commemorates his sacrifice with Bible verse John 15:13: "Greater love hath no man than this, that a man lay down his life for his friends."

⬆ Back on land after the disaster, three of the surviving stewards, including Frederick Dent Ray (left) and two unidentified men, posed together.

THE DECK CREW

On the deck of the *Titanic*, approximately four dozen seamen performed the daily work needed to keep a ship running, including maintaining equipment, standing watch, steering the ship and cleaning windows. Six members of the deck crew served as lookouts, taking bone-chilling two-hour shifts in the crow's nest 90 feet above water. (They did their job without binoculars, later a source of controversy in government inquiries.) During the evacuation of the ship, Officer Charles Lightoller sent six crewmen down to the portside lower deck gangway to open the doors and establish a pick-up point for lifeboats. Those six were never seen again— possibly killed by water crashing in through the doors they attempted to open. Most seamen aboard the ship survived, however, with many taking charge of lifeboats.

THE VICTUALLING DEPARTMENT

The largest subgroup of the *Titanic*'s staff, the Victualling Department comprised anyone whose job was to take care of guests. "Steward" was the most common title, with over 300 of them cleaning bedrooms, delivering room service, doing laundry and even shining shoes. Twenty stewardesses, who served female passengers, represented nearly all of the women crew

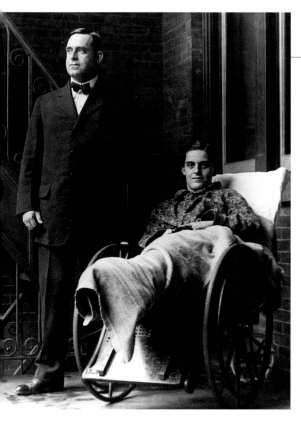

↑ Saloon steward Thomas Whiteley broke his leg when he was caught in one of the ropes as the lifeboats were being lowered.

members aboard the ship. Victualling was led by purser Hugh McElroy, a charismatic man who would often join passengers for dinner. Mostly male and employed for low wages, members of the Victualling Department were low on the priority list for lifeboats. Of the more than 400 workers in Victualling, fewer than 100 survived.

THE ENGINEERS

Thanks to their highly specific skill sets, a team of 35 engineers was the highest-paid group of crew members aboard the *Titanic*. Given that the ship was on its maiden voyage, their

work to make sure everything was running smoothly was considered especially important. They were responsible for monitoring and maintaining the engines, boilers and other machinery, as well as managing the firemen, greasers and coal trimmers whose labor kept the ship running. While not a single engineer survived the shipwreck to tell their tale, the men are remembered as heroes: They remained working below deck to keep the ship's electricity running as it sank, allowing the evacuation to take place.

THE ORCHESTRA

Like the restaurant staff, the orchestra members aboard the *Titanic* weren't White Star employees. Rather, they worked for a British firm that contracted musicians out to luxury liners. For most of the voyage, they played as two separate groups: one a quintet, the other a violin/cello/piano trio that played exclusively at first-class eateries À la Carte and Café Parisien. However, they will always be remembered as a collective, as they gathered to play one final concert when the ship began to sink. Some say they kept playing until the very end, although the exact tune remains unknown. Back in his hometown of Colne, England, bandleader Wallace Hartley's funeral procession was attended by tens of thousands of onlookers. *

↑ After the *Titanic* sank, the surviving crew members were interviewed as part of a U.S. Senate inquiry in New York and Washington.

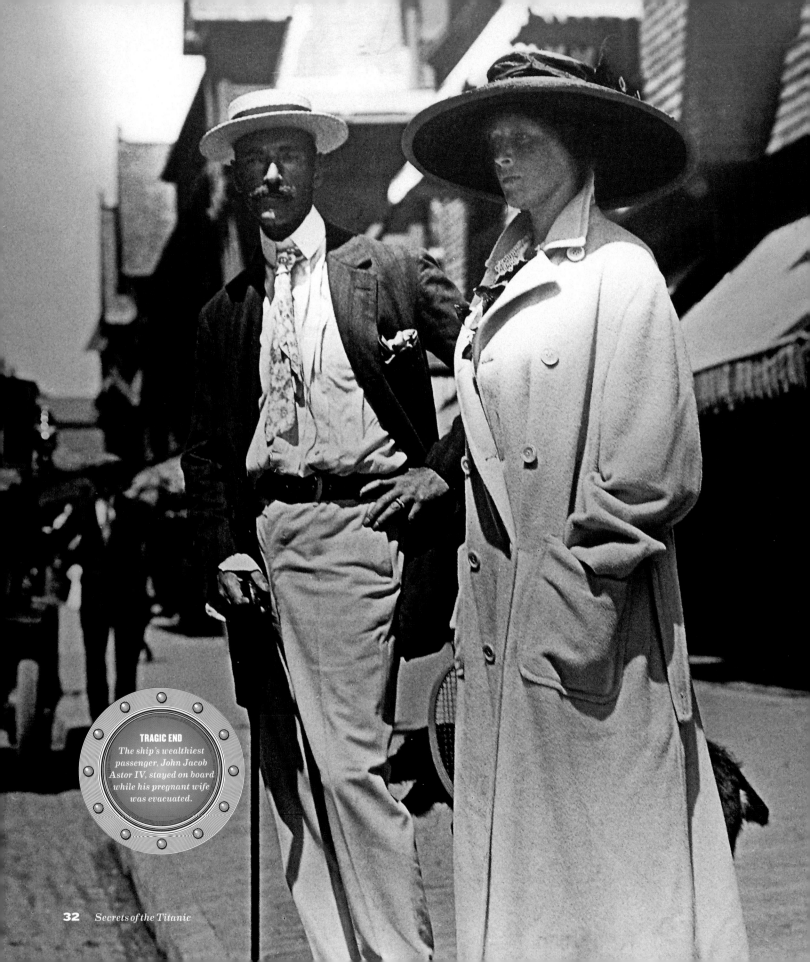

TRAGIC END
The ship's wealthiest passenger, John Jacob Astor IV, stayed on board while his pregnant wife was evacuated.

WHO'S WHO ON THE SHIP

THE STORIES OF THE TITANIC'S PASSENGERS ARE AS FASCINATING AS THE TRAGEDY THAT CHANGED—OR TOOK—THEIR LIVES.

The Movie Star

DOROTHY GIBSON

VITALS Born in Hoboken, New Jersey, on May 17, 1889. Died in Paris on Feb. 17, 1946.

CLAIM TO FAME One of the world's first movie stars, Gibson began her career as a Broadway chorus girl in her teens and later found success as a model, posing for such magazines as *The Saturday Evening Post* and *Ladies' Home Journal*. The popularity of these illustrations led to a contract at Éclair Studios in Fort Lee, New Jersey, in 1911. Almost overnight, Gibson became one of the highest-paid actresses in the world, but the work was grueling, and her personal life was chaotic. She was having an affair with Jules Brulatour, an Éclair producer who was twice her age and married with three children. In March 1912, the exhausted Gibson embarked on a European vacation with her mother, Pauline. After three weeks in Venice, they booked first-class return tickets on the *Titanic*, which they boarded in Cherbourg, France.

THE TRAGEDY At 11:40 p.m., after Gibson retired to the stateroom that she shared with her mother, she heard what she called "a long drawn, sickening crunch." Though she wasn't

"SUDDENLY THERE WAS A WILD COMING TOGETHER OF VOICES FROM THE SHIP AND WE NOTICED AN UNUSUAL COMMOTION AMONG THE PEOPLE ABOUT THE RAILING," GIBSON SAID OF THE SINKING. "THEN THE AWFUL THING HAPPENED, THE THING THAT WILL REMAIN IN MY MEMORY UNTIL THE DAY I DIE.... NO ONE CAN DESCRIBE THE FRIGHTFUL SOUNDS."

particularly concerned, she went to investigate. "As I started to walk across the boat, I noticed how lopsided the deck was," she said. Alarmed, she went back to tell her mother, with whom she escaped in Lifeboat No. 7—the first to be lowered on the starboard side—at 12:45 a.m. "I'll never ride in my little gray car again!" Gibson repeatedly screamed, referring

to a gift that Brulatour had given her before she'd left for Europe.

THE AFTERMATH Shortly after Gibson returned to New York, she wrote the script for *Saved From the Titanic*, a movie about the tragedy in which she starred as herself. Although the film was a huge hit, the process of reliving the events traumatized the actress, who soon abandoned her career and devoted herself to Brulatour.

In the spring of 1913, Gibson was driving to her lover's house on Long Island when she lost control of her "little gray car" and struck a married couple. The man died; the woman suffered serious injuries. When the public learned that the car belonged to Brulatour, he divorced his wife and married Gibson. By 1919, the relationship had soured. After divorcing Brulatour, Gibson moved to Paris with her mother.

For reasons that have never been entirely explained, during World War II, Gibson was imprisoned in a series of Nazi concentration camps and was later recruited to spy on the Allies. After the war ended in 1945, Gibson moved into the Ritz Hotel in Paris, where she died, probably of a heart attack, on Feb. 17, 1946.

SHOOTING STAR
A *fellow passenger on the* Titanic *called Gibson "the most beautiful girl."*

The Kidnapped Children

MICHEL AND EDMOND NAVRATIL

VITALS Michel Jr. was born on June 12, 1908, and died on Jan. 30, 2001. Edmond was born on March 5, 1910, and died on July 7, 1953.

CLAIM TO FAME In April 1912, Marcelle Navratil brought her sons, Michel (age 3) and Edmond (age 2), to spend Easter weekend with their father—her ex-husband, Michel—at his home in Nice, France. When she returned to pick them up, she was shocked to discover they had been kidnapped. Unbeknownst to Marcelle, 31-year-old Michel had taken the children on the *Titanic*, booking second-class tickets under the name Louis F. Hoffman and calling his boys Lolo and Louis.

A Slovakian native who had moved to Nice to become a tailor, Michel Sr. met Marcelle, who was 16 at the time, in 1906. A year later, the couple married, but it soon became apparent they were mismatched—she was artistic and emotional, while he was practical and deliberate. Worse, relatives claimed Marcelle was cheating on Michel and squandering his money. Whatever the reason, Michel Sr. felt that it was best to take his children to America in search of a better life.

"HE DRESSED ME VERY WARMLY AND TOOK ME IN HIS ARMS," MICHEL SAID OF HIS FATHER ON THE NIGHT OF THE SINKING. **"A STRANGER DID THE SAME FOR MY BROTHER. WHEN I THINK OF IT NOW, I AM VERY MOVED. THEY KNEW THEY WERE GOING TO DIE."**

At first, the trip appeared to be a grand adventure for the boys. "I remember looking down the length of the hull—the ship looked splendid," young Michel later said. "My brother and I played on the forward deck and were thrilled to be there. One morning, my father, my brother and I were eating eggs in the second-class dining room. The sea was stunning. My feeling was one of total and utter well-being."

THE TRAGEDY On the night of April 14, the Navratil boys were sleeping in their cabin when their father woke them up, dressed them warmly and took them to the deck. Michel helped other passengers (he even tied 12-year-old Madeleine Mellinger's new shoes) until Collapsible Lifeboat D, the last boat to be launched, became available. Second Officer Charles Lightoller was helping the boys on board when Michel Sr. whispered something into his eldest son's ear. The boy then turned to Lightoller and saluted him. Collapsible Lifeboat D left the *Titanic* at 2:05 a.m.

After being rescued by the *Carpathia*, fellow survivor Margaret Hays took the boys under her wing. She even brought them to her apartment when they reached New York. ("Where's papa?" asked Edmond, and Michel Jr. replied: "He's gone.") After Hays gave an interview about the children to a newspaper, their story became front-page headlines. Soon, it seemed that everyone had heard about the "Orphans of the *Titanic*"—including, as it turned out, their mother.

Given free passage from Nice to New York on a White Star Line ship,

Marcelle was reunited with her sons on May 16. It was a joyful event, but the boys had grown attached to Hays and were sad to leave New York. "You will never forget this beautiful young lady, will you?" Marcelle asked Michel Jr. "No indeed," the child said. "She is my good friend."

The next day, they returned to France on the *Oceanic*. Michel's body was later found floating in the Atlantic.

THE AFTERMATH Over time, the world forgot about the Navratil brothers. Michel became a student of philosophy and Edmond became an interior designer and architect—until he died at age 43, a victim of the ill health he'd suffered since he'd been a prisoner of war in World War II.

As Michel grew older, long-buried memories of the *Titanic* tragedy returned—including the words his father had whispered in his ear on the sinking ship: "My child, when your mother comes for you, as she surely will, tell her that I loved her dearly and still do," he'd said. "Tell her that I expected her to follow us, so that we might all live happily together in the peace and freedom of the New World."

Michel Jr. died in 2001; he was the last male survivor of the "unsinkable" ship.

The Wealthiest Man

JOHN JACOB ASTOR IV

↕ About four months after escaping the sinking on Lifeboat No. 4, Madeleine Astor gave birth to her fatherless son, John Jacob Astor VI, who was dubbed "The *Titanic* Baby."

VITALS Born July 13, 1864, in Rhinebeck, New York. Died April 15, 1912, in the Atlantic Ocean.

CLAIM TO FAME One of the wealthiest men in the world, Astor was the scion of the Gilded Age's most socially prominent American family. Although he was heir to a vast real estate and fur-trading fortune, Astor was something of a dilettante who wrote a science fiction novel, *A Journey in Other Worlds,* and patented several odd inventions—including a bicycle brake and "a vibratory disintegrator."

In the summer of 1910, following an acrimonious divorce from Ava Lowle Willing, the mother of his first two children, Astor met 18-year-old Madeleine Force in Bar Harbor, Maine. A whirlwind courtship led to marriage in September 1911, spurring condemnation from both the Astors and society at large.

On January 24, 1912, the couple tried to escape the growing criticism by traveling to Europe on the *Olympic.* They were accompanied by their beloved Airedale, Kitty, and their friend Margaret Brown, who later became known as "The Unsinkable Molly Brown." (For more on Brown, see page 48.) During the vacation, Madeleine became pregnant. After she started suffering from severe morning sickness, the trio cut the trip short and booked first-class return tickets on the *Titanic.*

THE TRAGEDY On the night of April 14, Madeleine retired early to her cabin.

At 11:40 p.m., she was awakened by a jolt. Though Astor was quick to reassure her that everything was fine, he nevertheless went to the bridge, where Captain Edward Smith told him the ship had struck an iceberg. Astor returned to his wife, fitted her with a life vest, and brought her on deck, where he helped her into Lifeboat No. 4. Because of her "delicate condition," Astor asked Second Officer Charles Lightoller if he could accompany his wife, but Lightoller refused, and Lifeboat No. 4 was lowered at 1:45 a.m.

Both Astor and his dog went down with the ship. Survivor Philipp Mock claimed he saw Astor hanging on to a raft with journalist William Thomas Stead. "Their feet became frozen, and they were forced to release their hold," he said. "Both were drowned." On April 22, Astor's body was found floating in the Atlantic by the recovery ship *Mackay-Bennett.*

THE AFTERMATH In the course of a year, Madeleine Astor had become a bride, a widow and an heiress, having inherited $100,000 and a $5 million trust fund after her husband's death. But there was a significant catch: Astor's will stipulated that his wife would lose the fund entirely if she remarried.

Love triumphed over money—for a while—before Madeleine married her childhood sweetheart, William Karl Dick, on June 22, 1916. The union produced two sons, but the couple divorced in 1933. Four months later, 39-year-old Madeleine married handsome 24-year-old Italian boxer Enzo Fiermonte, who repeatedly demanded money from his wife and beat her mercilessly when she refused. They divorced in 1938.

Increasingly depressed, Madeleine died in Palm Beach, Florida, on March 27, 1940. Although the official cause of death was heart failure, many of her friends suspected that she had overdosed on sleeping pills, either accidentally or intentionally. At the time, Madeleine was 47 years old—the same age that John Jacob Astor IV had been when he went down on the *Titanic.*

The President's Friend

MAJ. ARCHIBALD BUTT

VITALS Born Sept. 26, 1865, in Augusta, Georgia. Died April 15, 1912, in the Atlantic Ocean.

CLAIM TO FAME A journalist and veteran of the Spanish-American War, Maj. Archibald Butt served as adviser to President Theodore Roosevelt and his successor, William Howard Taft. Over time, Taft developed an almost neurotic reliance on Butt, who accompanied the president on 220 stops in 58 days through 28 states during a preelection campaign in 1911. "Do you wonder that our nerves have been disintegrated and our innards are all upside down?" the major wrote to his sister-in-law Clara.

In the spring of 1912, the overworked 45-year-old was suffering from exhaustion and chronic ill health. Though he hoped to recuperate with a vacation in Europe, Taft only consented to the trip after Butt's friend and housemate, the artist Frank Millet, swore that he would accompany the major, making sure that Butt would return in time to join the president at the Republican National Convention that June.

It seems likely that Butt and Millet were lovers. Although Millet

was married, he'd had a same-sex affair with the poet Charles Warren Stoddard, and Butt was an opera-loving, dandified bachelor with an extremely strong attachment to his mother (qualities that, at the time, were often associated with homosexuality). The men boarded the *Titanic* at Southampton, having booked separate first-class cabins,

although they may have slept in the same bed—discreetly, of course.

THE TRAGEDY On the night of April 14, Butt attended a dinner party in honor of Captain Edward Smith. He spent most of the evening talking with socialite Marian Thayer, confessing that—despite the vacation—his nerves remained fried. He was filled with anxiety about the upcoming presidential election and "did not know how he was going to stand the rushing life he was returning to," Thayer later said. She understood his fragile mental state: Her husband, John, suffered from depression. (So did her son, Jack, who survived the *Titanic* but died by suicide in 1945.)

After dinner, Butt and Millet were playing cards in the first-class smoking room when the *Titanic* struck the iceberg. After being reassured that the ship was safe, the men kept on playing cards—until 12:45 a.m., when it became clear something was terribly wrong. (People were screaming, and water was filling the listing ship.) The men headed for the deck, where they began helping women and children into lifeboats. Butt was particularly vigilant. When a panic-

 Maj. Butt (far left) was often called upon by President Taft (pictured here, center, at a 1912 garden fete) for advice.

"WHEN THE ORDER TO TAKE TO THE BOATS CAME, HE BECAME AS ONE IN SUPREME COMMAND. YOU WOULD HAVE THOUGHT HE WAS AT A WHITE HOUSE RECEPTION, SO COOL AND CALM WAS HE," SAID SURVIVOR RENÉE HARRIS.

stricken man tried to jump into a boat, the major grabbed him by the neck and jerked him violently backward. "Sorry," he said, "women will be attended first or I'll break every damn bone in your body."

Survivor Renée Harris later recalled Butt comforting her as she settled into Collapsible Lifeboat D. "He helped me find a space, arranged my clothing about me, stood erect, doffed his hat and smiled and said goodbye," she said. "And then he stepped back to the deck, already awash. As we rowed away, we looked back, and the last I saw of him he was smiling and waving his hand to me.... He was a soldier to the last...one of God's greatest noblemen." Millet's body was later recovered. Butt's was never found.

THE AFTERMATH On April 17, *The Baltimore Sun* reported that President Taft had given up all hope of finding Butt alive after the tragedy. Eulogizing his friend and colleague at a memorial service in Washington, D.C., he broke down in tears and could not continue.

The Broadway Producer

RENÉE HARRIS

LOST LOVE
"I have had four marriages—but really only one husband." Renée said of Henry.

Her Husband Went Down with the TITANIC

The Widow of the Celebrated Theatrical Producer Henry B. Harris, Herself One of the Last to Leave the Ship, Looks Back at That Night of Horror Twenty Years Ago

by RENÉ HARRIS

VITALS Born June 15, 1876, in Washington, D.C. Died Sept. 2, 1969, in New York City.

CLAIM TO FAME Renée was the wife of Henry Harris, one of New York's top theatrical producers and the man who had built Broadway's Hudson Theater. But she was far more than just a spouse. "I never take an important step without consulting Renée," Henry once said, adding, prophetically, as it turned out: "If anything happened to me, she could pick up the reins." The couple had just finished a four-month European vacation when they boarded the *Titanic* in Southampton and settled into their first-class cabin. Renée was 36, and her husband was 45.

THE TRAGEDY On the night of April 14, Renée slipped on the greasy remains of a tea cake that someone had dropped on the *Titanic*'s fore grand staircase and landed at the base of the stairs, fracturing her right elbow. When the ship hit the iceberg, Renée and Henry were awake and playing cards in their cabin, as she couldn't sleep because of the injury. Though Renée didn't feel the collision, she noticed the clothes in her closet had begun swinging. "So I said, 'We're going awfully fast to have my dresses sway like that—much too fast among icebergs.'" Just then, the ship's engines ground to a halt.

Even after the Harrises realized that the *Titanic* was doomed, Renée refused to leave her husband. In fact, they were still on deck in the ship's last moments when Renée was approached by an angry Captain Smith. "My God, woman!" he shouted. "Why aren't you in a boat?"

"I won't leave my husband," she replied. "Can he be saved, if I go?"

"Yes, there are plenty of rafts in the stern," the captain lied, "and the men can make for them if you women give them a chance."

When Henry tried to convince Ida Straus, the wife of Isidor, co-founder of Macy's department store, to take Renée with her in Collapsible Lifeboat D, Ida said, "I won't leave my husband. I will go where he goes."

Then Isidor turned to Renée. "We've been together all these years, and when we must go we will go together," he said. "You are very young, my dear. Life still holds much for you. Don't wait for my wife."

Renée probably would have ignored him, if Henry hadn't thrown her to a sailor. "Catch my wife," he said. "Be careful, she has a broken arm!"

Renée was soon lifted into Collapsible Lifeboat D. "God go with you," Isidor said.

"No, God is not with me," Renée thought. "He is with you and my beloved."

At 2:05 a.m., Collapsible Lifeboat D was lowered from the ship. Fifteen minutes later, the *Titanic* sank with 1,500 people—including Henry and the Strauses—still on board.

The bodies of Ida and Henry were never found. Isidor's was recovered.

⬆ Harris became a leading Broadway producer in her own right after the loss of her husband.

THE AFTERMATH "For months after the sinking of the *Titanic*, I was in a dreadful state of nerves and thought I would never be able to concentrate upon anything again," Renée said. "Then one memorable day I recalled the words of Mr. Harris: 'You are a better businessman than I.'" That became painfully obvious when Renée discovered that Henry was more than $400,000 in debt. "I knew then what I was going to do," she said. "I was going to carry on his work and make the theater a monument to his memory."

Renée became America's first female theatrical manager and producer, but she lost a fortune in the Crash of 1929. She was forced to sell the Hudson Theater and by the 1940s, she was living in a welfare hotel.

Renée married three more times, but Henry remained the love of her life. "He spoiled me for any other man in the world," she said. Renée later became close friends with Walter Lord, author of 1955's *A Night to Remember*, about the *Titanic* tragedy. She chose to call it "A Night to Forget."

The Philandering Hero

BENJAMIN GUGGENHEIM

VITALS Born Oct. 26, 1865, in Philadelphia. Died April 15, 1912, in the Atlantic Ocean.

CLAIM TO FAME The fifth of seven sons born to mining magnate Meyer Guggenheim, 46-year-old Benjamin boarded the *Titanic* at Cherbourg, France, with his valet, Victor Giglio; his chauffeur, René Pernot; a mysterious woman named Léontine Pauline Aubart; and her maid, Emma Sägesser. The group had spent eight months in Paris, where 24-year-old Aubart worked as a nightclub singer known as "Ninette." She was also the last of Guggenheim's many mistresses.

Despite having a wife, Florette, and three daughters at home in New York City, Guggenheim, who was known as "the Silver Prince," had a reputation as quite the playboy. In 1901, he had quit his father's firm to live off his own investments, leaving him free to travel, collect art and indulge in extramarital adventures. Though all of Meyer Guggenheim's sons were known for philandering, Ben was "the most extravagant in his amorous divagations," according to his nephew, Harold Loeb, "even introducing them into his own home."

THE TRAGEDY When the ship hit the iceberg, Guggenheim and Giglio were sound asleep. In fact, they remained blissfully unaware of the unfolding tragedy until Steward Henry Etches awakened them and urged them to put on life vests. At first, Guggenheim scoffed ("This will hurt," he said), but

↑ Guggenheim's wife, Florette (center), leaving White Star Line's New York City office, where she went seeking news of her husband just after the tragedy. In front of her are her friends Mr. and Mrs. DeWitt Seligman.

he and Giglio eventually complied. They headed to the boat deck, where they helped Aubart and Sägesser board Lifeboat No. 9. As the boat was lowered from the ship at 1:20 a.m., Guggenheim said, "We will soon see each other again! It's just a repair. Tomorrow the *Titanic* will go on again."

It was an honorable thing to say, but Guggenheim knew it was a lie. Returning to their suite, he and Giglio removed their life vests and changed into formal evening wear before returning to help people on the boat deck. When Etches saw the men in their finery, he said, "What's that for?"

"We've dressed up in our best and are prepared to go down like gentlemen," said Guggenheim. Then he asked Etches to do him a favor. "If anything should happen to me," he said, "tell my wife in New York that I've done my best in doing my duty." Later, he gave a message to another steward: "Tell my wife I played the game straight to the end and that no woman was left on board because Ben Guggenheim was a coward. Tell her that my last thoughts will be of her and our girls." With that, he lit a cigar and continued helping people into boats.

"On the deck there was no commotion," Aubart later said. "Every one of

> **"I AM WILLING TO REMAIN AND PLAY THE MAN'S GAME IF THERE ARE NOT ENOUGH BOATS FOR MORE THAN THE WOMEN AND CHILDREN."**

them a perfect gentleman—calmly puffing cigarettes and cigars and watching the women and children being placed in the boats.... Those Englishmen, still with cigarettes in mouth, facing the death so bravely that it was all the more terrible." As promised, Guggenheim and Giglio went down with the ship as gentlemen. Their bodies were never found.

THE AFTERMATH Aubart and her maid were rescued by the *Carpathia* and taken to New York, where they emerged traumatized and impoverished. The singer couldn't speak English, and had no money to return to France. Worse, she could no longer rely on the support of her wealthy lover, and the gifts he had given her were lost with the ship. "I had in my cabin jewels worth £4,000 as well as many trunks of dresses and hats," Aubart later said. "Nothing could be taken with me." Aubart died in France on Oct. 29, 1964, at age 77. *

STRONG SPIRIT
Socialite Margaret
("Molly") Brown
was known for her
outsize personality
and heart.

HEROES AND VILLAINS

SOME OF THE MEN AND WOMEN ON THE ILL-FATED VESSEL
SELFLESSLY SAVED LIVES, WHILE OTHERS MADE RECKLESS
—AND EVEN DELIBERATELY DESTRUCTIVE—DECISIONS.

HEROES

Margaret Brown

Later known as "The Unsinkable Molly Brown," the Denver socialite famously helped other passengers Into lifeboats before taking control of Lifeboat No. 6, which she helped row. On the *Carpathia*, she nursed injured survivors and stayed on the ship until passengers were reunited with relatives in New York City. Through it all, she never lost her sense of humor. "Water was fine and swimming good," she wrote to her attorney after the tragedy.

Thomas Andrews

Once he became aware that the ocean liner's sinking was "a mathematical certainty," the *Titanic*'s designer tirelessly worked to help other passengers into the lifeboats. Even after the boats were gone, Andrews tried to save people from drowning by throwing deck chairs into the water for them to grab on to. He reportedly went down with the ship, while staring at *Plymouth Harbor*, a painting that hung above the fireplace in the first-class smoking room.

Captain Arthur Rostron

Hearing the *Titanic*'s distress signals in the early morning on April 15, the *Carpathia*'s captain headed toward the sinking ship, 58 miles (about four hours) away. Soon after reaching the *Titanic*'s last reported position at 4 a.m., Rostron saw a green flare from Lifeboat No. 2. The first survivors came aboard at 4:15 a.m.; Second Officer Charles Lightoller, the last survivor, was rescued at 8:30 a.m. Rostron's prompt response saved hundreds of lives.

The Countess of Rothes

Born Lucy Noël Martha Dyer-Edwardes, the countess faced the sinking with a quiet heroism. She calmed panicked passengers in Lifeboat No. 8 and stoically helped row when it became obvious that the men on board were mostly inexperienced and ineffective. At one point, the countess even managed the tiller. After the *Carpathia* arrived in New York, she assisted passengers who had lost everything and had nowhere to go.

Wallace Hartley

The *Titanic*'s bandleader, Hartley was a violinist who tried to keep passengers calm by playing with the other members of the ship's string ensemble as lifeboats were loaded into the Atlantic Ocean. According to many survivors' accounts, the musicians kept at it—playing "Nearer, My God, to Thee"—until the unsinkable ship plunged into the sea. Although the musicians all perished, Hartley's violin and its case were later recovered.

Captain Edward Smith

The *Titanic*'s captain ignored ice warnings, increased the ship's speed instead of slowing it down, and failed to issue an "abandon ship" order, meaning many passengers didn't know the ship was doomed until it was too late. "Captain Smith is ultimately responsible for all the failures of the command structure on board; nobody else can take the blame," said Paul Louden-Brown of the *Titanic* Historical Society.

J. Bruce Ismay

The *Titanic* was the brainchild of Ismay, the president of the White Star Line, and it also proved the cause of his undoing. A passenger on the ship's maiden voyage, he boarded Collapsible Lifeboat C and escaped while women and children were left behind. As a result, he was widely condemned as a coward and pilloried in the press as "J. Brute Ismay." Consumed with self-loathing and guilt, he spent the rest of his life as a recluse.

Lady and Sir Cosmo Duff-Gordon

A successful fashion designer, Lady Duff-Gordon and her husband escaped from the *Titanic* on Lifeboat No. 1. Although the boat had been built to hold 40 people, only 12 were on board. At one point, Cosmo gave some of the crew members money, claiming it was an act of charity. But some said it was actually a bribe instead. Fearing that the lifeboat would be overrun, Cosmo wanted to avoid helping people who were drowning nearby.

Captain Stanley Lord

On the night of the tragedy, the captain of the SS *Californian* was awakened at least twice by his crew members, who said they'd seen white flares in the sky. Lord dismissed these as "company rockets," messages that ships from the same company use to recognize each other. In fact, they were distress flares—reportedly eight in total—from the *Titanic*. The *Californian* was only 20 miles away from the doomed ship and could have saved hundreds of lives if it had responded.

Jack Phillips

The *Titanic*'s chief wireless operator was undeniably overworked on the night of April 14, trying to process a backlog of messages caused by malfunctioning equipment. Nevertheless, he failed to pay sufficient attention to ice warnings from neighboring ships. One of them was never delivered to the bridge. The final—and most dire—warning was essentially ignored, a fatal oversight and the principal cause of the tragedy that followed.

her today everybody takes notice
of her through the Teddy Bear. There
is a Concert on Board tomorrow
night in aid of the Sailors Home
& she is going to sing so am I
well the Sailors say we have had
a wonderful passage up to now
there has been no tempest, but
God knows what it must be
when there is one, this mighty
expanse of water. No land in
sight & the Ship rolling from
side to side is very wonderful

LETTERS FROM THE *TITANIC*

ONLY A FEW MISSIVES ARE KNOWN TO HAVE BEEN WRITTEN
ON BOARD. HERE ARE EXCERPTS FROM SOME OF THEM.

April 10, 1912

KATE BUSS

Second-class passenger Buss wrote to her brother, Percy, as the *Titanic* traveled from Southampton, England, to Queenstown, Ireland—the ship's last port of call. The mention of "new paint" refers to the fact that the *Titanic* had recently been painted (the flowers that were brought on board in Southampton were supposed to disguise the smell). Buss escaped the wreck and eventually found her way to San Diego, where she married her fiancé less than a month later. Her letter sold at an auction for almost $35,000 in 2018.

I've been quite alright—but now feel dead tired & more fit for bed than anything. Have to go to dinner-tea in half an hour, Percy.... The first-class apartments are really magnificent & unless you had first seen them you would think the second class were the same.... I was advised to eat well so had a good lunch.... No sign of sea sickness yet—I mustn't crow.... The only thing I object to is new paint so far.... Must clear & have a wash now. Will pop this in the post in case I'm sea sick tomorrow.

MUSIC TO HER EARS
Kate loved hearing the ship's orchestra—and noted that the cellist often smiled at her.

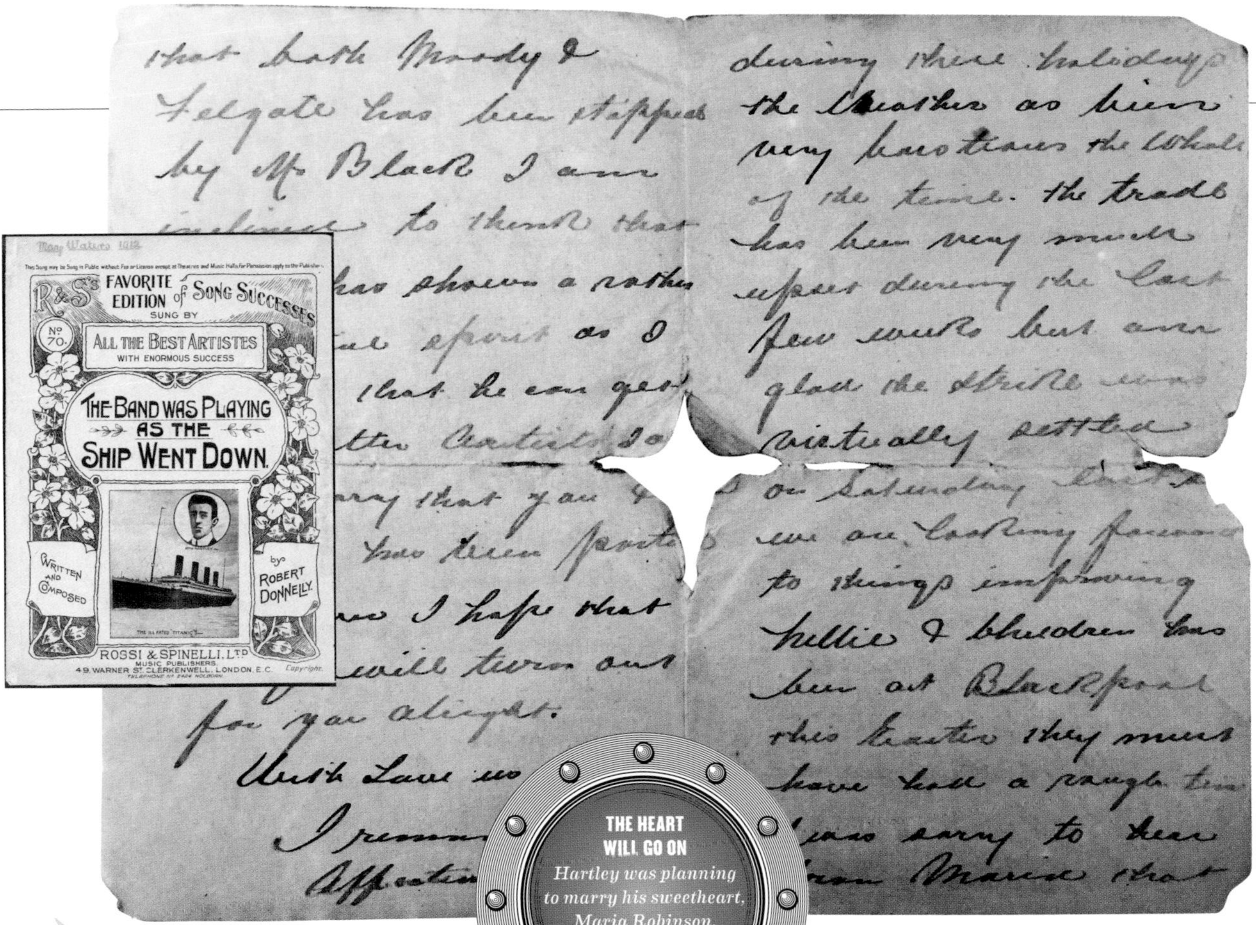

The sheet music cover and handwritten letter images appear here.

April 10, 1912

WALLACE HARTLEY

The bandleader who played with his group of musicians as the *Titanic* sank, and who died in the tragedy, wrote this letter to his parents on the first day of the voyage. His mention of "money" refers to expected tips. In 2013, the letter sold at auction for a reported $140,000.

Just a line to say we have got away all right. It's been a bit of a rush but I am just getting a little settled. This is a fine ship & there ought to be plenty of money on her. I've missed coming home very much & it would have been nice to have seen you all if only for an hour or two, but I couldn't manage it. We have a fine band & the boys seem very nice. I have had to buy some linen & I sent my washing home today by post. I shall probably arrive home on the Sunday morning. We are due here on the Saturday. I'm glad mother's foot is better.

THE HEART WILL GO ON
Hartley was planning to marry his sweetheart, Maria Robinson, in the summer of 1912.

DELAYED MAIL
"It was a very strange feeling," said a Simpson descendant of seeing the letter at auction.

April 11, 1912

DR. JOHN EDWARD SIMPSON

One of the *Titanic*'s doctors who went down with the ship, Simpson wrote this letter to his mother in Belfast, Ireland. It was mailed from Queenstown. The mention of the *Olympic* refers to the *Titanic*'s sister ship. The letter was thought to be lost until it showed up in a New York auction catalog in 2012. It sold for $35,000 to a benefactor who returned it to Simpson's descendants.

I travelled from Liverpool on Monday by the 12 o'c train & arrived on board at 10pm feeling pretty tired. I am very well & am gradually getting settled in my cabin which is larger than my last. This seems all the time as if it were the Olympic *& I like it very much....*

April 13, 1912

ALEXANDER OSKAR HOLVERSON

Holverson, a salesman, had been vacationing with his wife before they boarded the *Titanic* as first-class passengers in Southampton. Found on Holverson's body when it was retrieved from the Atlantic, this letter is the only one written on board the *Titanic* that was actually delivered to its recipient, Holverson's mother, after the ship went down. In 2017, it sold at auction for $166,000—a record price.

We had good weather while we were in London. It is quite green and nice in England now. This boat is giant in size and fitted up like a palacial [sic] hotel. The food and music is excellent and so far we have had very good weather. If all goes well we will arrive in New York Wednesday A.M. I am sending you a postcard of the ship and also a book of postcards showing the inside.... Mr. and Mrs. John Jacob Astor is [sic] on this ship. He looks like any other human being even tho he has millions of money. They sit out on deck with the rest of us and are very democratic.

April 14, 1912

ESTHER HART

Written by second-class passenger Hart, it's the only letter known to have been penned on April 14, the *Titanic*'s last day, and perhaps the last written on the ship. It was discovered in the pocket of the coat that Hart's husband, Benjamin, gave her before she climbed into the lifeboat. Although Benjamin died in the tragedy, Hart and her daughter, Eva, survived. The letter sold at auction for about $150,000 in 2014.

As you see it is Sunday afternoon and we are resting in the library after luncheon.... This morning Eva and I went to church and she was so pleased they sang "Oh God our help in ages past" that is her Hymn she sang so nicely.... There is to be a concert on board tomorrow night in aid of the Sailors' Home and she is going to sing so am I.

Well, the sailors say we have had a wonderful passage up to now. There has been no tempest, but God knows what it must be when there is one. This mighty expanse of water, no land in sight and the ship rolling from side to side...I shall never forget it. It is very nice weather but awfully windy and cold.... *

FIRST-CLASS AREAS
No expense was spared in making sure the posh rooms appealed to the upper-class passengers.

THE LAP OF LUXURY

TAKE A PEEK AT THE LUSH LIVING ABOARD
THE WORLD'S MOST LAVISH SHIP.

"The *Olympic* and the *Titanic* are not merely ships: They are floating towns, with all the improvements and conveniences that are associated with cities," the *Ulster Echo* wrote of the ocean liners in 1911. Located on seven of the *Titanic*'s 10 decks (labeled A to G), the finest of these features were reserved for first-class passengers, who enjoyed luxurious state rooms, Turkish baths, promenades...even a mechanical camel. Freezers on the lower deck were stocked with fresh produce and cut flowers, while kitchens overflowed with rich foodstuffs, more than 21,000 pieces of cutlery and 3,000 dishes—many custom-made.

No detail escaped the exacting eyes of the ship's builders and designers. White Star Line president J. Bruce Ismay worried that the mattresses on the *Olympic*, the *Titanic*'s sister ship, were too "springy," so he made sure the *Titanic*'s were suitably firm. Even after the ship was on its way to New York, designer Thomas Andrews obsessed over such minutiae as hat hooks (too many screws) and the pebble-dashing in the private promenades (too dark). But in the end, the *Titanic* was far greater than the sum of its parts. "She was a caravanserai of marvels; a mighty treasure house of beauty and luxurious ease," according to an article in the *Daily Graphic*. "What a place in which to dream!"

Here, a seven-deck tour of the ship's most rarefied amenities.

↑ A rendering of the first-class smoking room shows *Plymouth Harbor*—the painting the *Titanic*'s designer, Thomas Andrews, was staring at when the ship went down—above the fireplace.

The Social Spaces

THE LOUNGE

Decorated in Louis XV Versailles style, the A Deck lounge was one of the *Titanic*'s most elegant—not to mention ostentatious—rooms. Paneled in English oak inset with musical and floral motifs, it was serviced by its own bar and filled with bronze sconces, cozy tables, and chairs upholstered in green-and-gold velvet. A replica of Diana of Versailles, an ancient Roman statue, sat on the fireplace mantelpiece. A library offered popular new books. "When talk becomes monotonous," read a White Star Line promotional pamphlet, "we may here indulge in bridge and whist, or retire with our book or our letters to one of the many quiet retreats which reveal themselves to the thoughtful explorer."

THE READING AND WRITING ROOM

Next to the lounge, this Georgian-style room was reserved for women, and decorated with delicate, "feminine" colors: a red carpet, white walls, pink silk curtains. An airy space with views of the portside promenade, it was the favorite room of Harland & Wolff's chairman, Lord Pirrie, according to a 1911 article in *The Shipping World*. "Fireplace, bow windows and the furnishings generally convey an idea of a retreat in some country house amid 'haunts of ancient peace,'" it read.

THE SMOKING ROOM

This Georgian-style lounge at the aft end of A Deck was the exclusive haunt of men—*gentlemen*, that is—

First-class female passengers enjoyed their own space in the elegantly decorated reading and writing room, where they sipped tea, wrote letters or just gossiped.

who drank cocktails, played cards, smoked cigars and gambled. (Four professional card sharps were reportedly on board the night the *Titanic* sank.) Upholstered chairs, mahogany paneling with mother-of-pearl inlay, a coal-burning fireplace and back-lit stained-glass windows created a simultaneously intimate and elegant ambiance. The most famous object in the room, Norman Wilkinson's painting *Plymouth Harbor,* hung over a coal-burning white marble fireplace.

THE GRAND STAIRCASE

Stretching 60 feet from A Deck to E Deck, the *Titanic*'s magnificent forward grand staircase was the navigational hub for first-class passengers and the undisputed highlight of the ship's interior. The 16-foot-wide oak structure featured gold-plated light fixtures, hand-carved paneling and oil paintings on every landing. During the day, sunlight streamed from a ceiling dome, which was illuminated with electricity at night.

The top flight of the staircase was reached through the first-class entrance off the boat deck and led down to A Deck. On the wall of the half-flight, an elegant clock was flanked by carved wooden figures representing "Honor and Glory Crowned with Time," while a statue of a cherub carrying a lamp perched on a pedestal at the landing. Every level of the staircase had a foyer, the largest of which served as the entrance to the dining saloon's reception room on D Deck.

The Restaurants

THE RECEPTION ROOM AND DINING SALOON

The white-paneled reception room contained an Aubusson tapestry, Chesterfield chairs, a floor covered with Axminster carpet, and a Steinway piano. The ship's most popular spot for predinner drinks and postprandial coffee, it was also the site of the traditional English Teas that were held (accompanied by music from the ship's band) every day at 4 p.m. At the end of the reception room, double doors led into the white-enameled, Jacobean-style dining saloon.

The largest room on the *Titanic*, the dining saloon was 113 feet long and—like the reception room—as wide as the ship, about 92 feet. Every evening, up to 532 diners enjoyed 11-course meals in the expansive space. The saloon's final supper menu featured Oysters à la Russe, Calvados-Glazed Roast Duckling and Chocolate Painted Eclairs. "The first-class passenger sits down to dinner in the splendid saloon, with its windows of cathedral-gray glass, and the attendants switch on cunningly hidden electric lights on the outside," *The Standard* wrote on April 10, 1912. "The effect is naturalness itself."

À LA CARTE RESTAURANT

The À la Carte Restaurant on B Deck was decorated in Louis XVI style, with French walnut panels, bay windows, crystal chandeliers and an Axminster carpet "in a delicate vieux rose," according to one breathless account. Fresh carnations and pink silk–shaded lights adorned the tables, while food was served on custom-made Royal Crown Derby china. Instead of multiple courses served on set schedules, patrons could order food à la carte (what else?) from 8 a.m. to closing at 11 p.m.—a unique approach to dining at the time. On the night of the tragedy, first-class passenger Mahala Dutton Douglas watched fellow patrons feasting on "caviar, lobster, quail from Egypt, plover's eggs, and hothouse grapes and fresh peaches."

CAFÉ PARISIEN

Adjacent to the restaurant, the more casual Café Parisien was particularly popular with the ship's younger passengers. "This café has the appearance of a charming sunlit verandah, tastefully decorated in French trelliswork with ivy and other creeping plants, and is provided with small groups of chairs surrounding convenient tables," *Shipbuilder* magazine wrote at the time.

One of the only elements on the ship that was not also echoed on the *Olympic*, the Parisien was designed to suggest a Parisian sidewalk café. As such, it had large picture windows that allowed guests to enjoy views of the sea while dining—an unprecedented feature on ocean liners at the time. "The Parisian Café is quite a novelty and looks very real," one British

STAIRWAY TO HEAVEN
Each landing on the Titanic's *fore grand staircase had cozy seating nooks.*

passenger wrote to his wife. "It will no doubt become popular amongst rich Americans." The food was rich, too: On the night of the disaster, the café's menu included oysters, salmon, roast duck, sirloin of beef, pâté de foie gras, peaches in Chartreuse jelly, and vanilla and chocolate eclairs.

THE VERANDAH CAFÉ

This was actually two cafés—one on each side of the ship, aft of the smoking room on A Deck. Also known as the Palm Courts because they resembled a traditional palm court—an atrium with palm trees— the cafés served snacks rather than meals and had white wicker chairs, ivy-covered trellised walls and high arched windows. The portside café was for smokers, while the starboard side was for nonsmokers, making it a favorite spot for mothers to spend time with their children.

The Accommodations

THE STATE ROOMS

The *Titanic*'s first-class rooms were a hodgepodge of decorative styles (Italian Renaissance, Louis Quinze, Regency and Old Dutch, just to name a few). Though all first-class accommodations had telephones and heaters, the most expensive offered wardrobes and private baths, which were fabulously rare at the time. (Most *Titanic* passengers, including many in first class, shared public bathrooms.) The accommodations varied

↑ There are no color photos of the *Titanic*, but obsessives have established the hues in the design scheme and offer guides for mixing them—just in case you want to give your home the feeling of a doomed ocean liner. (Colors include "White Star Buff" and "Yellow Chromate.")

widely in price, with the cheapest—a simple berth—costing the equivalent of today's $3,500.

THE PROMENADE SUITES

The ship's four so-called "Millionaire Suites"—the most expensive accommodations available on the *Titanic*— cost well into the five figures when calculated in today's dollars. Two of these were on C Deck, but the most luxurious (and expensive) accommodations were the Promenade Suites located on B Deck and featured their own private 50-foot-long promenades. J. Bruce Ismay traveled in the Promenade Suite on the *Titanic*'s port side, while its three-room

equivalent on the starboard side (reportedly the ship's most expensive) was occupied by Charlotte Wardle Cardeza, who was a notoriously disagreeable Philadelphia heiress.

After surviving the disaster, Cardeza sued the *Titanic*'s owners for $177,352.75 (in 1912 dollars!) to compensate for the clothes, money and jewelry she'd lost when her 20 boxes, trunks and suitcases vanished into the Atlantic Ocean that fateful night. Among the items reported missing: "Box with flowers for hair, Box with combs for hair, Box of set combs for hair Wanamaker's, 2 cakes Vera Violette soap" and "Jewelry, Stickers, Monte Carlo."

⬆ The *Titanic*'s Verandah Cafés and Turkish baths (the cooling room is shown at right) were virtually identical to those featured on its sister ship, the *Olympic*.

The Athletic Facilities

THE GYMNASIUM

The *Titanic*'s state-of-the art gym offered rowing machines, stationary bikes and a motorized camel, which supposedly offered the same dubious health benefits gained from riding the real thing. The young fitness instructor Thomas W. McCawley gave weight-training and boxing lessons. Passengers could also visit the squash racquet court on G Deck.

THE TURKISH AND SWIMMING BATHS

Located on F Deck, the Turkish baths featured a temperate room, a "hot" room kept at 200 degrees Fahrenheit, a steam room, two shampooing rooms and a cooling room. The comparatively spartan swimming bath was a 6-foot-deep heated saltwater pool. ⁎

TRAINING DAY
Thomas W. McCawley, the ship's fitness instructor (in black), died at his post.

How the Third-Class Passengers Lived

⬆ A reproduction of a third-class cabin was part of a French exhibit to commemorate the 100th anniversary of the ship's sinking.

The *Titanic* was a ship of extremes, with the vast wealth of its millionaires contrasting sharply with the poverty of the people who traveled in the vessel's bowels. About 700 of the *Titanic*'s passengers were in third class—more than in first and second classes combined—and many were poor emigrants who bunked, sometimes six to a room, in narrow, overcrowded cabins. Although private baths were rare on ships at the time (even the *Titanic*'s second- and first-class passengers had to share bathrooms), there were only two bathrooms in third class: one for men and one for women.

Still, the lower decks weren't as grim as they're often made out to be. "Passengers accustomed to using outhouses, or who had never tasted refrigerated milk or sampled the delights of ice cream, found themselves partaking of such wonders in a significantly upgraded standard of living," according to the authors of *On a Sea of Glass*, a history of the tragedy. "Most third-class passengers were accustomed to working with their hands—often in appalling conditions—or had previously been employed in the service of others. But in their dining saloon they were treated to full-service attention by stewards who did their best to provide for their needs and wishes."

In addition to the saloon, third-class passengers had their own general room, a smoking room and access to the poop deck, where they could get fresh air. "I often noticed how the third-class passengers were enjoying every minute of the time: a most uproarious skipping game of the mixed-double type was the great favourite, while in and out and roundabout went a Scotchman with his bagpipes," second-class passenger Lawrence Beesley wrote in his memoir, *The Loss of the SS Titanic.*

Still, Beesley was aware of the class divide on the ship, specifically noting a third-class passenger who had bought a second-class ticket for his wife. "He would climb the stairs leading from the steerage to the second deck and talk affectionately with his wife across the low gate which separated them," he wrote. "Whether they ever saw each other on the Sunday night is very doubtful: he would not at first be allowed on the second-class deck, and if he were, the chances of seeing his wife in the darkness and the crowd would be very small, indeed." In the end, Beesley recognized very few of the people he'd seen playing happily in steerage among the ship's survivors on the *Carpathia*.

CAFÉ SOCIETY
A glimpse of what it might have looked like to dine in the Titanic's Verandah Café

WHAT THEY ATE AND DRANK

ON A SHIP KNOWN FOR ITS EXTRAVAGANCE, FOOD
WAS NO EXCEPTION—FROM THE RARE WINES OF
FIRST CLASS TO THE ICE CREAM IN STEERAGE.

↑ First-class diners in a scene from 1953's *Titanic* (above). At right: There was no such thing as a "light lunch" on board the ship.

R.M.S. "TITANIC"

APRIL 14, 1912.

LUNCHEON.

CONSOMMÉ FERMIER   COCKIE LEEKIE
FILLETS OF BRILL
EGG À L'ARGENTEUIL
CHICKEN À LA MARYLAND
CORNED BEEF, VEGETABLES, DUMPLINGS

FROM THE GRILL.
GRILLED MUTTON CHOPS
MASHED, FRIED & BAKED JACKET POTATOES
CUSTARD PUDDING
APPLE MERINGUE   PASTRY

BUFFET.
SALMON MAYONNAISE   POTTED SHRIMPS
NORWEGIAN ANCHOVIES   SOUSED HERRINGS
PLAIN & SMOKED SARDINES
ROAST BEEF
ROUND OF SPICED BEEF
VEAL & HAM PIE
VIRGINIA & CUMBERLAND HAM
BOLOGNA SAUSAGE   BRAWN
GALANTINE OF CHICKEN
CORNED OX TONGUE
LETTUCE   BEETROOT   TOMATOES

CHEESE.
CHESHIRE, STILTON, GORGONZOLA, EDAM,
CAMEMBERT, ROQUEFORT, ST. IVEL,
CHEDDAR

Iced draught Munich Lager Beer 3d. & 6d. a Tankard.

Growing up in Wausau, a small town in northern Wisconsin, author Veronica Hinke first became interested in the *Titanic* when she learned about Daniel Coxon, a popcorn vendor who had lived in the nearby town of Merrill. A third-class passenger who had traveled to London to visit his family, Coxon died in the disaster. "I was intrigued by how a man who lived in the next town had been a passenger on a splendid ship like the *Titanic*," she says.

In 2011, as the 100th anniversary of the disaster approached, Hinke began researching the Champagnes, wines and cocktails served on the *Titanic*,

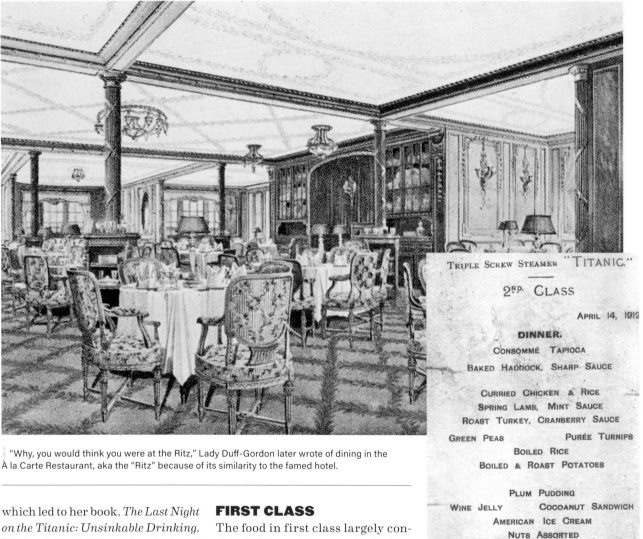

"Why, you would think you were at the Ritz," Lady Duff-Gordon later wrote of dining in the À la Carte Restaurant, aka the "Ritz" because of its similarity to the famed hotel.

TRIPLE SCREW STEAMER "TITANIC."

2ND CLASS

APRIL 14, 1912

DINNER.

CONSOMMÉ TAPIOCA

BAKED HADDOCK, SHARP SAUCE

CURRIED CHICKEN & RICE
SPRING LAMB, MINT SAUCE
ROAST TURKEY, CRANBERRY SAUCE

GREEN PEAS   PURÉE TURNIPS
BOILED RICE
BOILED & ROAST POTATOES

PLUM PUDDING
WINE JELLY   COCOANUT SANDWICH
AMERICAN ICE CREAM
NUTS ASSORTED
FRESH FRUIT
CHEESE   BISCUITS
COFFEE

"No effort had been spared to give even second-class passengers the best dinner that money can buy," a passenger said.

which led to her book, *The Last Night on the Titanic: Unsinkable Drinking, Dining & Style*. "I love the stories of the people aboard the *Titanic*," Hinke says. "And every food story, at its core, is about the people."

Here's a closer look at what the passengers ate and drank on those doomed final days.

FIRST CLASS

The food in first class largely consisted of the cuisine popularized by Auguste Escoffier, who revolutionized French cooking by simplifying recipes for the home cook. "The White Star Line hired Italian restaurateur Luigi Gatti as a concessionaire to run the French dining rooms aboard

⬆ Among the offerings at the ship's final first-class feast: raw oysters and assorted hors d'oeuvres, followed by more than a half-dozen courses.

the *Titanic*," Hinke says. "The food they prepared was similar to what was served in the finest restaurants during the Edwardian years." As a result, it was time-consuming to prepare and consume. "In first class, 10-course dinners would last four and five hours," says Hinke, adding that the menu on the *Titanic*'s last night included oysters, foie gras and consommé Olga (ordinary consommé made with port wine and other ingredients including celery, carrots, leeks and gherkins). "Spring ingredients were ubiquitous in first class," she adds. "There were spring peas, asparagus, new potatoes, rhubarb, lamb and mint sauce, and more."

SECOND CLASS

Compared to the cuisine in first class, the food in second and third classes was relatively basic, according to Hinke. "One of the most telling examples of the difference between first and second classes is the dessert," she says. "In second class, there was American ice cream,

↑ The first-class dining saloon was positioned between the second and third funnels to ensure the smoothest possible ride.

↑ The second-class dining facilities and service were still considered opulent for the era.

while in first class there was French ice cream. The difference? French ice cream includes egg yolks, which creates a richer ice cream, with a bit more of a yellow color." There was less variety in the offerings in second class, too. "There were two soups in first class on the *Titanic*'s last night— consommé Olga and cream of barley," she says. "In second class, there was only the consommé."

THIRD CLASS

In third class, tripe, oatmeal and gruel were on the menus, along with hearty soups and stews. Although these dishes may sound basic and unappealing, they were much better than what third-class passengers would have been served on any other liner. "While first class was far and away much more elegant and formal, the accommodations and food in third class and second class were superior to those in similar classes on other Edwardian-era steamships at the time," Hinke says. *

COUNTDOWN BEGINS

It took only 37 seconds for the ship to strike the iceberg after it was sighted by the lookout.

CHAPTER 2

The Fatal Night

*Despite numerous warnings, the ocean liner sailed at
high speed through an ice field, setting off the deadly disaster
that would cost more than 1,500 lives.*

FOR THE RECORD
*Wireless operators
were often lower-class
young men who hoped
to escape dead-end
careers on land.*

THE LAST DAY ON THE *TITANIC*

ON APRIL 14, 1912, THE LUXURY PASSENGER LINER MET
ITS DATE WITH DESTINY WHEN IT COLLIDED
WITH AN ICEBERG IN THE FRIGID NORTH ATLANTIC.
HERE, A LOOK AT THE TRAGIC FINAL NIGHT.

On the cold, sunny morning of April 14, 1912, the White Star Line's RMS *Titanic* was in the fourth day of its maiden voyage from Southampton, England, to New York City.

It was Sunday, so the ship's captain, Edward J. Smith, held a traditional Church of England service in the first-class dining saloon at 10:30 a.m. About half of the 329 ship's first-class passengers attended, singing "Oh God, Our Help in Ages Past" and "Eternal Father, Strong to Save" from the *White Star Hymnal*. (At the time, no one would have thought it ominous that the latter hymn included the verse "Oh hear us when we cry to thee, for those in peril on the sea.") After the service ended, the stewards began preparing the saloon for luncheon at 1 p.m. "Sunday was a perfect day," passenger Arthur Peuchen later said.

Given the clear weather and unusually calm sea, most passengers would have been surprised to learn that danger lurked ahead: It was a bad year for icebergs in the North Atlantic, the result of a particularly mild winter. Though spring ice was common around the Grand Banks near Newfoundland, Canada, 300 bergs had been spotted in the shipping lanes that month alone. "Not for 50 years, the old sailors tell us, had so great a mass of ice and icebergs at this time of the year been seen so far south," passenger Archibald Gracie later wrote.

Many of these bergs were directly in the *Titanic*'s path—a fact passing ships

TICKING CLOCK
It only took 160 minutes for the Titanic to sink once it struck the iceberg.

TITANIC

Wireless technology was relatively unproven when the *Titanic* sailed, but the fact that it saved so many lives made its inventor, Guglielmo Marconi, a hero.

bridge—except, inexplicably, the *Amerika*'s (to this day, no one knows what happened to it). After receiving the *Baltic*'s message, Captain Smith put it in his pocket instead of giving it to his officers. Shortly afterward, he gave it to J. Bruce Ismay, the White Star Line's managing director, who read it without saying a word.

A 62-year-old veteran sailor, Smith was unconcerned about potential dangers. "I never saw a wreck and never have been wrecked, nor was I ever in any predicament that threatened to end in disaster of any sort," he'd once said. Besides, everyone knew that the *Titanic* was "unsinkable." Several passengers later recalled the captain saying the ship could be cut crosswise in three places and each piece would float. The ship's designer, Thomas Andrews, boasted that the worst that could happen was a collision that would flood two of the ship's 16 watertight compartments—and even then, he said, the *Titanic* would stay afloat.

Smith was so confident of his vessel's seaworthiness that, instead of slowing it down (a standard precaution near ice), he sped it up. "The captain had each day improved upon the previous day's speed, and prophesied that, with continued fair weather, we should make an early arrival record for this maiden trip," Gracie recalled. "In the 24 hours' run ending the 14th, according to the posted reckoning, the ship had covered 546 miles, and we were told that the next 24 hours would see even a better record made."

repeatedly pointed out. That Sunday, Jack Phillips and Harold Bride, the wireless operators who manned the *Titanic*'s Marconi Room, received seven ice warnings. The first was sent at 9:12 a.m. from the Cunard liner *Caronia*, which reported "bergs, growlers and field ice," followed by news of "much ice" from the *Noordam*, a Holland America liner, at 11:47 a.m. At 1:49 p.m., the German liner *Amerika* reported "two large icebergs." Five minutes later, the captain of the *Baltic*, a fellow White Star ship, noted "icebergs and large quantity of field ice" about 250 miles ahead of the *Titanic*.

Following protocol, Phillips and Bride passed the warnings to the

That Sunday, the first-class lunch menu featured Fillets of Brill, Egg à l'Argenteuil, Galantine of Chicken, Apple Meringue and Custard Pudding. After the plates were cleared from the table, many passengers noted that the temperature had dropped precipitously and that the wind had risen. Everyone was "restlessly searching for a warm place," passenger Margaret (Molly) Brown later wrote. "The comfortable chairs in the lounge held but a few, as a shaft of cold air seemed to penetrate every nook and corner, and chill the marrow."

Ignoring the bad weather, passenger Marian Thayer convinced her friend Emily Ryerson to join her on the promenade deck. Ryerson and her husband, Arthur, had boarded the *Titanic* in Cherbourg, France, having cut their Paris trip short after learning that one of their sons had died in a car accident in Pennsylvania. Around 6 p.m., Emily and Marian settled into chairs and watched the sky turn pink. It was, Ryerson said, "Very cold but perfectly beautiful."

Before long, the women were approached by Ismay, who had heard of the Ryersons' loss and given them an extra stateroom. "I hope you are comfortable and all right," he said. Despite Ismay's largesse, Ryerson was annoyed by his attentions, especially when he took the *Baltic*'s message from his pocket and announced: "We are in among the icebergs.... We are not going very fast, 20 or 21 knots, but we are going to start up some

The *Titanic*'s Café Parisien (top), and an Adams-style stateroom similar to what would have been found among the first-class accommodations on the ship.

new boilers this evening." In fact, Ismay said that he hoped to reach New York ahead of schedule. (Later, Captain Smith approached Ismay in the smoking room and asked him for the *Baltic*'s message, saying that he wanted to post it in the officers' chart room. He never did.)

At 6:53 p.m., the sun began to set in what one passenger called "a wide blood-red band from the ship's side to the horizon" as the *Titanic* entered the area where the Labrador Current meets the warmer Gulf Stream waters. Suddenly, the wind disappeared and the temperature plunged to 43 degrees Fahrenheit.

Inside the ship, workers attached the last three of the 24 principal boilers to the engine, increasing the speed just as the first-class passengers headed to dinner—an elaborate

> ## "I ENJOYED MYSELF AS IF I WERE IN A SUMMER PALACE ON THE SEASHORE…. THERE WAS NOTHING TO SUGGEST THAT WE WERE ON THE STORMY ATLANTIC OCEAN."
>
> *- Archibald Gracie -*
> FIRST-CLASS PASSENGER

THE HIGH LIFE
The grand staircase's A Deck landing (left) and passengers enjoying the boat deck.

affair, to say the least. The women were "shining in pale satins and clinging gauze," passenger Helen Candee noted. They were also decked in priceless jewels retrieved from the ship's safe—most notably the $250,000 pearl necklace belonging to Eleanor Widener, the American socialite who was hosting a dinner for Captain Smith that night.

At 7:15 p.m., the first officer, William Murdoch, asked the lamp trimmer, Samuel Hemming, to close the shuttle hatch. "We are in the vicinity of ice, and there is a glow coming from that," he said. "I want everything dark before the bridge." The stars were beginning to appear in the Eastern sky, but there was no moon, so visibility was crucial—especially since the ice warnings continued. At 7:22 p.m., Stanley Lord, captain of the

Leyland Line's *Californian*, warned of "three large bergs 5 miles to the southward of us"—only 50 miles away from the *Titanic*.

Meanwhile, the Wideners' dinner party was underway in the B Deck's À la Carte Restaurant. As the guest of honor, Captain Smith was seated at the head of the table, which was covered with pink roses and white daisies. Other invitees included Maj. Archibald Butt, an aide-de-camp of President William Howard Taft; socialites William and Lucile Carter; and Marian Thayer and her husband, John. As the ship's musicians played in the corridor, the diners discussed Wall Street, the upcoming presidential election, and the ship's ever-increasing speed.

Around 8:55 p.m., the captain excused himself and headed for the bridge, where he mentioned the frigid weather to Second Officer Charles Lightoller. "Yes, it is very cold, sir," Lightoller replied. "In fact it is only one degree above freezing."

"There is not much wind," the captain said.

"It's a flat calm as a matter of fact."

"A flat calm."

"Yes, quite flat," said Lightoller, who knew the lack of wind meant that no ripples of water would indicate potential icebergs ahead. Still, he wasn't terribly concerned, since icebergs could generally be seen from 1.5 to 2 miles away. "In any event," he said, "there will be a certain amount of reflected light from the bergs."

Strangely, there are no known photographs of the outfitted engine and boiler rooms on the *Titanic* or its sister ships. These images give a general sense of what the areas, the equipment and the workers would have looked like.

THE GREENLAND SHELF
Strong winds and global warming have accelerated the calving of icebergs in recent years.

The captain agreed, but advised Lightoller to slow the ship if conditions became hazy. "If in the slightest degree doubtful, let me know," he said. At 9:30 p.m., Smith left the bridge during the most crucial—and dangerous—part of the voyage.

Ten minutes later, Lightoller asked Sixth Officer James Moody to warn the lookouts, George Symons and Archie Jewell, to watch for "small ice" and "growlers," or low-floating bergs. Naturally, the men were already aware of the hazards. ("By the smell of it there is ice about," Symons had said to Jewell. "As a rule you can smell the ice before you get to it.") But the lookouts had no binoculars, which had inexplicably disappeared between Belfast and Southampton.

The *Titanic* was now near Cape Race in Newfoundland, Canada, where a wireless station gave the ship its first direct contact with North America. At 9:52 p.m., Phillips was frantically answering and relaying messages from Cape Race in the Marconi Room when he received the most important—and ominous—warning yet. It came from Stanley Adams, the wireless operator on the liner *Mesaba*. "Saw much heavy pack ice, and great number large icebergs, also field ice," he reported, indicating a 78-mile-long rectangular ice field that was directly in the *Titanic*'s path—in fact, the ship was already inside it.

"Received, thanks," Phillips replied.

"Stand by," Adams said, waiting for Phillips to confirm that he had passed the news on to the *Titanic*'s captain. But Phillips was preoccupied with the

"A splendid musician he was," said one of bandleader Wallace Hartley's colleagues, "and a better fellow you could not meet in a day's march. He was one of the best." Hartley had once told a friend that he would play "Nearer, My God, to Thee," if he were on a sinking ship.

Cape Race messages and Bride had already gone to bed, so the warning never reached the bridge.

It would prove to be a fatal mistake.

After dinner, the music from the band in the reception room mingled with the sound of "happy, laughing men and women constantly passing up and down those broad, strong staircases," as passenger Elizabeth Shutes later put it, "and the music went on and the ship went on." In the third-class general room, passengers danced as one man played his uilleann pipes. "The girls all loved" the music, one observer said—until someone spotted a rat. In the second-class dining saloon, almost 100 people sang hymns under the direction of the Rev. Ernest Carter, who told the story behind every song. Just before Marion Wright sang "Lead, Kindly Light," for instance, Carter explained that it had been inspired by a shipwreck in the Atlantic.

At 10 p.m., lookouts Frederick Fleet and Reginald Lee took over for Symons and Jewell in the crow's nest, and Lightoller turned the watch over to Murdoch, the first officer, saying that he estimated that they would reach the ice around 11 p.m.

Meanwhile, the stewards were turning off the lights in the third-class public rooms, and the hymn-singing ended with a rendition of "Stand Up, Stand Up for Jesus." Before the crowd dispersed, the Rev. Carter mentioned how secure everyone felt on such a large, stable ship and thanked the

> "THERE WAS NO MOON
> AND I HAVE NEVER
> SEEN THE STARS
> SHINE BRIGHTER; THEY
> APPEARED TO STAND
> RIGHT OUT OF THE SKY,
> SPARKLING LIKE CUT
> DIAMONDS.... IT WAS
> THE KIND OF NIGHT
> THAT MADE ONE FEEL
> GLAD TO BE ALIVE."
>
> *- Jack Thayer -*
>
> *TITANIC* SURVIVOR ON THE LAST NIGHT

ARTISTIC LICENSE
This period rendition ignores the fact that the impact with the iceberg was below the surface.

singers for their participation. "It is the first time that there have been hymns sung on this boat on Sunday evening," he said, "but we trust and pray it won't be the last."

One by one, the passengers began retiring to their rooms. "The quietness of the night was broken only by the muffled sounds that came to me through the ventilators of stewards talking and moving along the corridors," according to passenger Lawrence Beesley, who was reading in his room. "Nearly everyone was in their cabins, setting down for the long night. Some asleep in bed,

"GROSS CARELESSNESS. THE CAPTAIN KNEW WE WERE GOING INTO AN ICE FIELD, AND WHY SHOULD HE REMAIN DINING IN THE SALOON WHEN SUCH DANGER WAS ABOUT?"

- Arthur Peuchen -

FIRST-CLASS PASSENGER

others undressing. And others just down from the smoking room and still discussing many things."

At 11:07 p.m., the *Titanic* received the day's seventh—and final—warning. Once again, it came from the *Californian*'s Captain Lord, who had anchored his ship after being surrounded by ice just north of the *Titanic*. He asked his wireless operator, Cyril Evans, if there were any other vessels in the area.

Yes, Evans replied: "The *Titanic*."

"Better advise him we are surrounded by ice and stopped," Lord said. Despite the danger, Evans began his message with deceptive informality: "Say old man, we are stopped and surrounded by ice."

The news blasted into Phillips' earphones—the *Californian* was less than 20 miles away—and Phillips was irritated by what he thought was idle chitchat. "Shut up, shut up, I am busy!" he snapped. "I am working Cape Race." Evans did not repeat the warning. When his shift was over, he turned off his set and went to bed. No one took his place.

"It was a very strange night," Lord later said. "It was hard to define where the sky ended and the water commenced. There was what you call a soft horizon." Nevertheless, the *Titanic* was barreling into the ice field at 22.5 knots, or 25 miles an hour—its fastest speed yet.

At 11:40 p.m., about 400 nautical miles south of Newfoundland, lookout Fleet saw a massive iceberg looming above the water 500 yards away. "There is ice ahead!" he said,

ringing the alarm bell three times— a sign that there was something directly in the ship's path—and calling the wheelhouse from the crow's nest telephone.

"Is someone there?" he said when Sixth Officer Moody answered.

"Yes," Moody said.

"What do you see?"

"Iceberg straight ahead."

Moody relayed the information to First Officer Murdoch, who ordered the helmsman to turn "hard-a-starboard," meaning to the left. It was the worst thing he could have done. "Had the *Titanic* hit head-on, the ship would come to a shuddering stop, most people would have been knocked over, china's all over the place, pots in the kitchen are on the floor, boiling water everywhere," according to Claude

Daley, DSc, a professor of ocean and naval architectural engineering at Memorial University of Newfoundland. "They would clean up the mess, seal off the forepeak, carry on their way. And they would have gone home again."

To make matters worse, Murdoch ordered the engines to be reversed, which caused the ship to turn even more slowly. The crew waited in agony until the *Titanic* finally seemed

to pull away from the iceberg— "a close shave," Fleet thought—but the relief was premature: The ship had only missed the 10% of the berg visible above the water. Thirty-seven seconds after the initial sighting, a submerged spur of the 15,000-year-old iceberg scraped the starboard bow just below the waterline.

Inside the ship, the impact went virtually unnoticed. "There came to me what seemed nothing more than

an extra heave of the engines," passenger Beesley recalled. "Nothing else—no shock, no jar that felt like one heavy body meeting another.... No cry in the night, no alarm given, no one afraid."

Indeed, some passengers were gleefully kicking the ice around the decks; one ordered a waiter to add some of it to his highball, and another was given a chunk as a souvenir. Captain Smith rushed onto the deck from his cabin

FIVE PEOPLE WHO MISSED THE BOAT

J.P. Morgan
Financier
"Monetary losses amount to nothing in life," Morgan told *The New York Times* soon after the tragedy. "It is the loss of life that counts. It is that frightful death." Morgan knew what he was talking about—the *Titanic* was built with his money. The millionaire had planned to travel on the ship's maiden voyage but decided instead to stay in Aix-les-Bains, France, where he vacationed every year.

Guglielmo Marconi
Inventor
The inventor of the wireless radio was offered free passage on the *Titanic*'s maiden voyage but opted for the *Lusitania*: He had work to do, and he preferred the *Lusitania*'s stenographer. Although the *Titanic*'s wireless operators failed to relay important warnings from other vessels that night, its distress calls reached the *Carpathia*, which saved hundreds of survivors. The event made Marconi a hero.

behind the wheelhouse. "What have we struck?" he asked Murdoch.

"An iceberg, sir," Murdoch replied.

"Close the watertight doors."

"The watertight doors are closed, sir."

Awakening in his lavish suite, Ismay wondered why the engine had stopped. Slipping an overcoat over his pajamas, he headed to the deck, where Captain Smith told him the bad news: "We have struck ice."

"Do you think the ship is seriously damaged?" Ismay asked.

"I'm afraid she is," Smith replied.

Thomas Andrews, the ship's chief designer, was shocked to discover that the iceberg had sliced open nearly one-third of the ship, compromising six of its 16 watertight compartments. The *Titanic* could only survive the loss of three. The ship was going to sink. It was midnight. The *Titanic* had less than three hours to live. ✳

Lord William Pirrie
Chairman of Harland & Wolff

Pirrie reportedly wanted to travel on the ship's maiden voyage but he was sidelined by illness. If he had made the trip, he either would have died or (like his colleague J. Bruce Ismay) spent the rest of his life as a pariah: a man who had escaped on one of the lifeboats, even though he was partly responsible for the fact that there weren't enough of them.

Theodore Dreiser
Novelist

The writer had planned to take the *Titanic* but booked passage on the *Kroonland* instead because it was less expensive. "To think of a ship as immense as the *Titanic*, new and bright, sinking in endless fathoms of water," he wrote in his 1913 memoir, *A Traveler at Forty*. "And the two thousand passengers routed like rats from their berths only to float helplessly in miles of water, praying and crying!"

Milton Hershey
Candy Maker

In December 1911, Milton Hershey —the man whose name became synonymous with chocolate—was traveling in France when he wrote a $300 check to the White Star Line, a deposit toward a stateroom on the *Titanic*'s first voyage. When urgent business required his attention back home, he took an earlier trip on the German liner *Amerika*—one of the ships that later sent ice warnings to the *Titanic*.

HEAVY LOAD
About 400 tons of water per minute flooded into the ship after it hit the iceberg.

TITANIC SINKING TIME LINE

FROM THE EARLIEST CALLS FOR HELP, TO THE MOMENT
THE SHIP SLIPPED UNDER THE SEA, HERE'S A CLOSER LOOK
AT THE LAST HOURS OF THE ONCE MIGHTY VESSEL.

12:15 a.m.

Captain Edward Smith orders wireless operator Jack Phillips to send out the first distress signal from the *Titanic*'s Marconi Room. Phillips types out "CQD" (the international distress call), "MGY" (the *Titanic*'s call letters) and the ship's position. The *Frankfurt* and the *Titanic*'s sister ship, the *Olympic*, respond—but both are too far away to help. The Cunard liner *Carpathia* changes course to try to reach the sinking ship. Captain Smith orders the crew to get the lifeboats, boarding women and children first.

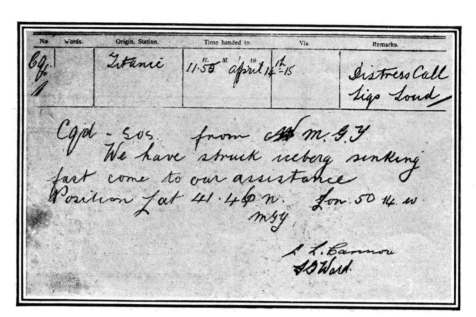

12:45 a.m.

The *Titanic*'s first lifeboat, No. 7, is launched as the ship's band plays on deck. Only 28 people are on board the lifeboat, though it can hold up to 65. The *Titanic* fires the first of a reported eight distress flares. The *Californian*, a ship about 20 nautical miles away, sees the flares—but inexplicably ignores them. Phillips sends out the first SOS signal in the history of the world.

12:55 a.m.

The second and third lifeboats, No. 5 and No. 6, leave the *Titanic*. A woman is injured when two men jump into boat No. 5. Lifeboat No. 6 is commandeered by Quartermaster Robert Hichens, who was at the helm when the *Titanic* struck the iceberg. His refusal to help other survivors—whom he calls "stiffs"—infuriates passenger Margaret (Molly) Brown, who threatens to throw him overboard.

1 a.m.

As Lifeboat No. 3 is lowered, water is seen at the base of the grand staircase, creating panic. In the Marconi Room, Phillips' distress calls grow increasingly desperate, noting the ship "cannot last much longer." Lifeboat No. 1 is launched with only 12 people aboard, although it can hold 40. (First-class passengers Sir Cosmo Edmund Duff-Gordon and his wife are blamed for bribing crewmen to avoid going back.)

1:20 a.m.
Lifeboat No. 10 is launched; it carries 9-week-old Millvina Dean, the youngest passenger, who eventually became the last living survivor. Lifeboat No. 9, on the stern starboard side, is lowered. One of the occupants is the mistress of American businessman Benjamin Guggenheim; he (along with his valet) later changes into formal attire, saying, "We've dressed up in our best and are prepared to go down like gentlemen."

1:10 a.m.
Lifeboat No. 8 is launched on the port side with only 28 people on board—including first-class passenger Lucy Noël Martha Leslie, the Countess of Rothes, who heroically helps steer. Isidor and Ida Straus are offered seats in the boat, but Isidor refuses to go before all women and children have been evacuated, and Ida won't leave her husband behind.

1:25 a.m.
Clearly unaware of the scope of the disaster, the *Olympic* radios: "Are you steering southerly to meet us?" The *Titanic* responds: "We are putting the women off in the boats." Lifeboat No. 12 is lowered.

1:30 a.m.

Several male passengers try to board Lifeboat No. 14, causing Fifth Officer Harold Lowe to fire his gun three times in warning. Phillips continues to send out distress calls: "Women and children in boats. Cannot last much longer." Lifeboat No. 13 is launched, followed by No. 15, which nearly lands on top of it.

1:45 a.m.

Lifeboats No. 2 and No. 11 are launched with about 20 and 50 people aboard, respectively. Madeleine Astor is helped onto No. 4 by her husband, John Jacob Astor IV, who stays behind as the boat is lowered.

1:35 a.m.

Lifeboat No. 16 is launched.

> ## "SUDDENLY, I SAW THE *TITANIC* GO DOWN, STRAIGHT UP, WITH HORRIBLE EXPLOSIONS AND EXCRUCIATING SCREAMS.... THERE WAS THEN A HUGE SWIRL, THEN SILENCE."
>
> - *George Rheims* -
> FIRST-CLASS PASSENGER

1:40 a.m.

Collapsible Lifeboat C is lowered. On it is White Star chairman J. Bruce Ismay (right), who is later pilloried for leaving women and children behind.

2 a.m.

The *Titanic*'s bow has sunk so low that the ship's propellers are now visible. Captain Smith releases the crew, saying, "It's every man for himself." Crewmen lower Collapsible Lifeboat D from the officers' quarters with more than 20 on board, leaving only three collapsible boats behind. As the *Titanic*'s bow goes under the water, Collapsible Lifeboat A is washed from the deck. Some 30 men climb onto the overturned lifeboat.

2:18 a.m.

The *Titanic*'s lights go out as the ship splits in two. The stern rises vertically out of the water, where it remains for a moment before plunging into the ocean. "A thin, light gray smoky vapor that hung like a pall just a few feet above the surface of the broad expanse of sea," Archibald Gracie later wrote in a memoir. "Cries more terrible than I had ever heard rang in my ears," said second-class passenger Charlotte Collyer.

2:17 a.m.

Phillips sends a final distress signal and manages to swim to overturned Collapsible Lifeboat B. He later succumbs to exposure.

2:20 a.m.

The *Titanic* is gone. Hundreds of people are dying in the freezing water, hundreds more are already dead, and about 710 survivors await rescue in the lifeboats, which could have saved up to 400 more. The U.S. puts the death toll at 1,517 passengers and crew, while the British estimate 1,503.

3:30 a.m.

The *Carpathia*—the so-called "Ship of Widows"—arrives in the area of the wreck. Eventually the survivors board and head for New York, which they reach on April 18.

HOW TO SURVIVE A SHIPWRECK

BOAT SAFETY HAS IMPROVED BY LEAPS AND BOUNDS SINCE THE LOSS OF THE TITANIC. BUT NO SHIP IS UNSINKABLE. NEXT TIME YOU'RE ON THE OPEN WATER, KEEP THESE TIPS IN MIND IN CASE DISASTER STRIKES.

GET NOTICED
Arrange rocks, branches or other objects on the land so rescuers can more easily spot you from the sky.

BE PREPARED

If you're captaining your own boat, you're responsible for your passengers' safety as well as your own. To start with, make sure that the combined weight of your occupants and equipment don't exceed your boat's capacity. From there, it's a matter of keeping the right equipment on board. A first-aid kit, a flashlight, a fire extinguisher, ropes and flares are all musts. Perhaps most important are life jackets—and not just a random assortment pulled from the shed. Each passenger should have access to a life jacket that fits properly.

If you're a passenger on a cruise ship: Enjoy! But listen carefully to the safety briefings at the beginning of your voyage, and familiarize yourself with your cabin's location in relation to emergency meeting points.

2 WEATHER THE SEA

Contemporary cruise liners are required to carry enough life rafts for all their passengers, so you likely won't have to defer entirely to women and children like so many *Titanic* passengers did. (If you do need to jump overboard, dive as far away as possible to escape getting sucked into the ship's wake.) On a smaller vessel, cling tightly to your capsized boat, a buoyant piece of equipment or whatever else you can hold. The key is flotation—swimming to shore is rarely the best option.

3 FIND RESOURCES

If you drift to land before you're rescued, set up for a hopefully very temporary stay. Even waterlogged clothes retain some warmth, so resist the urge to strip down. If you're stranded with companions, cuddle together to combine body heat. For shelter, build a lean-to from large branches, and fill in the gaps with leaves. Scavenge for food and fresh water. No matter how thirsty you are, drinking salt water will only dehydrate you further.

4 SIGNAL FOR HELP

Rescuers are surely on their way, and it's your job to help them find you. If you recovered flares in the wreckage, don't fire them off at random. Instead, wait for the passing of a ship or aircraft that could possibly see it. If you don't have flares, reflecting sunlight with a mirror or building a fire can also catch someone's attention. And when you're not building shelter or looking for food, spell out a giant "SOS" or "HELP" with stones.

5 GET PROPER CARE

Once you are safe back home, seek medical treatment. Depending on your situation, surviving a shipwreck can leave wounds both physical (impact injuries, hypothermia, malnutrition) and psychological (post-traumatic stress disorder). Take the time you need to heal with professional help.

LOVE AND LOSS
Items like this pocket watch—which belonged to a couple who perished together—were brought up from the wreckage.

CHAPTER 3

The Aftermath

The world reacted with shock as the full story of the ship's tragic end came to light—and would soon discover the heroism (and cowardice) of those aboard.

TITANIC LOST

Unparalleled Shipping Calamity

TRAGIC COLLAPSE OF A MAIDEN VOYAGE

REPORTED LOSS OF OVER 1,600 LIVES.

WOMEN AND CHILDREN SAVED.

675 Rescued by Lifeboats.

GRAPHIC DETAILS.

INTERESTING PHOTOGRAPHS.

"All the News That's Fit to Print."

The New York Times.

THE WEATHER

NEW YORK, TUESDAY, APRIL 16, 1912.—TWENTY-FOUR PAGES.

ONE CENT

TITANIC SINKS FOUR HOURS AFTER HITTING ICEBERG; 866 RESCUED BY CARPATHIA, PROBABLY 1250 PERISH; ISMAY SAFE, MRS. ASTOR MAYBE, NOTED NAMES MISSING

The Lost Titanic Being Towed Out of Belfast Harbor.

PARTIAL LIST OF THE SAVED.

CAPT. E. J. SMITH, Commander of the Titanic.

BREAKING NEWS

Papers around the country and the world were quick to report every detail they could get on the disaster.

The Daily Mirror

THE MORNING JOURNAL WITH THE SECOND LARGEST NET SALE.

No. 2,645. TUESDAY, APRIL 16, 1912. One Halfpenny.

DISASTER TO THE TITANIC: WORLD'S LARGEST SHIP COLLIDES WITH AN ICEBERG IN THE ATLANTIC DURING HER MAIDEN VOYAGE.

ONE ON BOARD WORLD'S GREATEST LINER SAFE AFTER COLLISION WITH ICEBERG IN ATLANTIC OCEAN

...NIC'S WIRELESS SIGNAL BRINGS VESSELS TO SCENE

LINERS IN PERIL FROM ICEBERG

LLOYD'S MESSAGE

MILES OF FLOES

SHOCKING THE WORLD

AS EARLY NEWS OF THE DISASTER ROLLED IN—SOME FACTUAL, SOME MISLEADING—REACTION TO THE SINKING OF THE TITANIC WAS ONE OF DISBELIEF.

THE TORONTO DAILY STAR
April 15

"The passengers of the *Titanic*, it is understood at the White Star offices here, will be taken to Halifax. The damaged liner will proceed to that port and there unship her passenger luggage.

"Mr. Mitchell, manager of the White Star office, left today to attend to the dispatch of passengers tomorrow, when it is expected they will arrive."

THE NEW YORK TIMES
April 16

"The White Star liner *Olympic* reports by wireless this evening that the Cunarder *Carpathia* reached, at daybreak this morning, the position from which wireless calls for help were sent out last night by the *Titanic* after her collision with an iceberg. The *Carpathia* found only the lifeboats and the wreckage of what had been the biggest steamship afloat."

THE BELFAST TELEGRAPH
April 16

"POSSIBLY MORE SURVIVORS: No information has been received from the liners *Parisian* or *Virginian* at the White Star offices, where it is still believed that many of the *Titanic*'s passengers are aboard these vessels."

THE WASHINGTON POST
April 16

"In a tangled maze of wireless messages that flashed first hope, then stupefying despair, to a waiting, nerve-strained nation, there was revealed last night an overwhelming tragedy of the ocean.

"In the black horror of a boundless midnight, the great steamship *Titanic*, with 2,200 passengers on board, crashed into an iceberg, and four hours later plunged deep to her grave off the banks of Newfoundland. The vessel was bound from Liverpool to New York, on her maiden voyage."

THE DAILY MIRROR
(BRITAIN)
April 16

"The majority of the 900 men forming the *Titanic*'s crew are either natives of Southampton or are domiciled at that port.

"The first half-pay notes given to the wives or dependents of the members of the *Titanic*'s crew became payable yesterday, and after receiving their money women gathered in small groups the Southampton dock gales, many of them with babies in their arms, and anxiously discussed the latest news respecting the liner."

LE PETIT JOURNAL
(PARIS)
April 16

"One dispatch said that they had hurried to save the women; another announced the departure of liners sent at full steam from New York to rescue the *Titanic*. But it was not known whether they had arrived in time and the rescuers' efforts had been successful, or if it had been a terrible disaster, similar to the sinking of [SS *La*] *Bourgogne*, if not more dreadful still."

THE TIMES DISPATCH
(RICHMOND, VIRGINIA)
April 16

"'Loss likely to total 1,800 souls,' the dispatch said…. It is hoped and believed here that this is an error, unless the *Titanic* had more passengers on board than had been reported. The list as given out showed 1,380 passengers and a crew of 860, or 2,170 persons in all. Deducting 675, the known saved, would indicate a loss of 1,495 persons."

THE SPHERE

AN ILLUSTRATED NEWSPAPER FOR THE HOME

With which is incorporated "BLACK & WHITE"

Volume XLIX. No. 640. | London, April 27, 1912. | Price Sixpence.

HOW THE TITANIC WENT DOWN

THE MODERN MESSENGER OF DEATH:

A typical bearer of the tidings concerning the

Le Petit Journal

LE PAQUEBOT "TITANIC"

DE LA COMPAGNIE ANGLAISE "WHITE STAR LINE"
est entré en collision avec un iceberg
PRÈS DE TERRENEUVE

Les 2.700 personnes qui étaient à bord
ont été sauvées

COMMENT LA FRANCE VERRA L'ÉCLIPSE DE SOLEIL
demain 17 Avril

Netes Politiques

PROPOS D'ACTUALITÉ

La science et le crime

Sur la ligne centrale

WAITING GAME

Because many of the survivors were on board the Carpathia, it took almost a week for reports to be verified.

The Times Dispatch

WHOLE NUMBER 18365. | RICHMOND, VA., TUESDAY, APRIL 16, 1912. | PRICE TWO CENTS

Titanic, Giant White Star Liner, Sinks After Collision With Iceberg on Her Maiden Voyage, and 1,800 Lives Are Reported Lost in World's Greatest Marine Disaster

WIRELESS CALLS SEND VESSELS RUSHING TO AID OF SEA COLOSSUS

Through the Night They Drive With Full Speed to Reach Titanic.

MEANTIME, WORLD WAITS IN AGONY OF SUSPENSE

THE TITANIC

OF ALL ON BOARD ONLY 675 KNOWN TO HAVE ESCAPED DEATH IN OCEAN

Those Rescued Mostly Women and Children, Who Were Taken Off in Boats.

BITS OF WRECKAGE ALL THAT IS LEFT OF GREAT VESSEL

COL. JOHN JACOB ASTOR IS AMONG DROWNED

FINANCIAL BLOW IS VERY SEVERE

CARRIED NOTABLE PASSENGER LIST

HAS $5,000,000 INSURANCE

OFFICIALS CONCEDE GREAT LOSS OF LIFE

PEOPLE ON SHIPS GET FIRST NEWS

STILL HOPING FOR BEST

ST. LOUIS POST-DISPATCH

HOME EDITION

Only Evening Paper in St. Louis With the Associated Press News Service.

VOL. 64. NO. 246. | ST. LOUIS, TUESDAY EVENING, APRIL 16, 1912—28 PAGES | PRICE ONE CENT

Last Sunday's Count of Want Ads
Post-Dispatch......7149
All............6011
Post-Dispatch Gain 384

1302 LIVES LOST WHEN "TITANIC" SANK; 868 SAVED

Carpathia Steaming to New York With Survivors; None on Other Ships

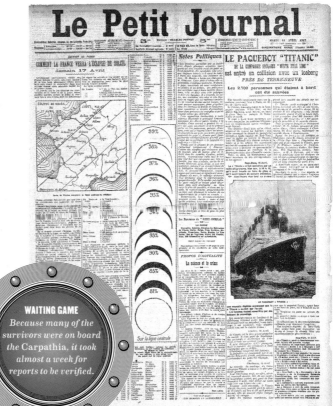

7 ST. LOUISANS ARE REPORTED SAFE ON BOARD CARPATHIA

ABOUT 2200 PERSONS ON TITANIC.

2-THIRDS WOMEN IN PARTIAL LIST OF THOSE RESCUED

Astor, Butt, Guggenheim and Many Other Famous Men Who Were on Board Not Mentioned Among Survivors—Money Loss Is $20,000,000.

EARLY ALERT
Telegraph operator David Sarnoff alerted the press about the Titanic's loss from his office in New York.

AN IMMEDIATE INVESTIGATION

BEFORE SURVIVORS OF THE TITANIC HAD EVEN REACHED
LAND, THE U.S. SENATE LAUNCHED AN INQUIRY
INTO WHAT HAD GONE SO HORRIBLY WRONG.

On April 15, 1912, a young man named David Sarnoff showed up to his job as a Marconi telegraph operator at Wanamaker's in New York City. John Wanamaker, the proprietor of the illustrious department store, had the wireless telegraphs installed in his stores with dual purposes: conducting company business and giving customers a chance to send messages of their own.

Sarnoff had picked up transmissions between the ships the *Olympic* and the sinking *Titanic* the night before. On this day, he kept his ears open for further communication pertaining to the incident. While vague news of the ship hitting the iceberg had already made the papers, it was unclear whether the ship had actually sunk, or even if any deaths had occurred. Late in the afternoon, Sarnoff overheard another message from the *Olympic,* this one to White Star Line's New York office.

Carpathia *reached* Titanic *position at daybreak. Found boats and wreckage only.* Titanic *foundered about 2:20 AM in 41.16 N. 50.14 W. All her boats accounted for. About 675 souls saved.* Leyland Line SS Californian *remaining and searching position of disaster.* Carpathia *returning to New York with survivors.*

"About 675 souls saved": With just over 2,200 on board, that would mean over 1,500 lives lost.

Sarnoff informed the press, and the news was on the front pages of

"THE COMMITTEE FINDS THAT THIS ACCIDENT CLEARLY INDICATES THE NECESSITY OF ADDITIONAL LEGISLATION TO SECURE SAFETY OF LIFE AT SEA."

- U.S. Senate Investigation Into Loss of **SS** Titanic *-*

evening editions within the hour. A crowd swamped the White Star office, demanding the names of survivors.

Two days later, the *Carpathia* still had not reached New York harbor. In Washington, D.C., Sen. William Alden Smith of Michigan read the latest news over breakfast. The world was clamoring for answers, and papers were doing their best to provide them. Smith noticed that they had all decided on Captain Edward Smith as their initial villain, claiming he had recklessly sped the ship through ice. But Smith had met Captain Smith years earlier, and the seafarer had struck the politician as anything but reckless. Something wasn't adding up.

So eager was Smith to take action that he interrupted the opening prayer at that morning's Senate ses-

sion. He proposed an investigative panel composed of members of the Committee of Commerce, including himself. The Senate approved the idea unanimously.

Smith hadn't planned to commence his investigation until the survivors reached land, but two concerning developments came to his attention the next morning. First, two boats sent by President William Howard Taft had successfully met the *Carpathia* out at sea, but those on the de facto rescue ship refused to hand over a full list of its passengers. Second, those two ships had intercepted a peculiar telegram from *Carpathia.*

To P.A.S. Franklin, White Star. Most desirable Titanic *crew should be returned home earliest moment possible. Suggest you hold* Cedric, *sailing her daylight Friday. Propose returning in her myself. —Yamsi*

The message contained a code, albeit one that was unraveled in seconds. "Yamsi" spelled backward was "Ismay"—as in White Star chairman Bruce J. Ismay, owner of the *Titanic.* He had survived the wreck, he was on the *Carpathia,* and he was clearly hoping to spend as little time as possible on American soil.

Smith immediately called the Oval Office, scheduling a noon meeting with President Taft in which he'd receive permission to subpoena Ismay and other British citizens who'd survived the shipwreck. The *Carpathia* was set to arrive in New York that

⬆ Michigan Senator William Alden Smith led the U.S.'s investigation into the *Titanic*'s untimely end, often asking deliberately simple questions so the crew would be forced to answer in equally plain language, and not technical jargon.

night, and Smith intended to be there to welcome it. When he and his fellow Senate investigators got to Union Station for their train, reporters who had learned of the Ismay telegraph met them with shouted questions. A narrative had emerged in the papers that Captain Edward Smith had been forced to accelerate through ice at Ismay's orders. Captain Smith, it was now known, had died in the wreck.

The senators arrived at the pier only moments after the *Carpathia* did. Smith boarded the ship, preparing to shoulder past whoever stood between him and Ismay. Hardly anyone did; the exhaustion and trauma of the wreck was evident on every face he saw. Finally Smith got to Ismay's temporary quarters, secluded away from the main part of the ship where rescued passengers had slept on floors and tables. On the door was written, "please do not knock."

Expecting to square off with a defiant, high-powered businessman, Smith had practiced a speech on the train ride to New York. But the Ismay he encountered was slumped over, shaking, and hollow-eyed—in even worse condition than other passengers Smith had seen. When the senator informed him that he'd be expected to testify in front of the committee, Ismay made no objections. He claimed that his telegraph requesting a quick return to England was not an attempt to evade accountability, but rather an effort to return British survivors to their families as quickly as possible.

The hearings began on Friday, April 19 at 9 a.m.—that is, less than 12 hours after Smith first confronted Ismay aboard the *Carpathia*. The public fascination with the shipwreck, which was especially pronounced in New York City, meant that the hearings would be anything but a dry governmental proceeding. They were hosted in a venue whose elegance rivaled that of the *Titanic*: the Waldorf-Astoria. Reporters and other spectators filled the hotel's East Room beyond capacity within minutes.

From his very first statement, Ismay sought to come across as open and transparent—the opposite of his portrayal in the media.

"In the first place, I would like to express my sincere grief at this deplorable catastrophe," he told the panel. "I understand that you gentlemen have been appointed as a committee of the Senate to inquire into the circumstances. So far as we are concerned, we welcome it. We court the fullest inquiry. We have nothing to conceal; nothing to hide."

He also refuted the idea that he had encouraged the ship's captain to blow through ice full speed ahead, as many papers were reporting. "I understand it has been stated that the ship was going at full speed," he said. "The ship never had been at full speed. The full speed of the ship is 78 revolutions. She works up to 80. So far as I am aware, she never exceeded 75 revolutions. She had not all her boilers on. None of the single-ended boilers were on."

↑ *Titanic* Captain Edward Smith (top) was blamed for his part in the crash; *Carpathia* Captain Arthur Rostron (center) was lauded for his rescue efforts. President William Taft (above) took an active interest in the hearings.

Ismay professing his own innocence was one thing, but his first real vindication came later that day during the testimony of Arthur Rostron, captain of the *Carpathia*. It was under Rostron's command that the crew of *Carpathia* rescued the survivors of the *Titanic*, making him one of the few heroes of the tragedy. He had no possible motive for giving the investigators a false account, so the audience was ready to take him at his word.

When Smith launched into a line of questioning about whether a ship's captain would take commands from its owner, Rostron emphatically rejected the possibility.

"At sea, immediately I leave port until I arrive at port, the captain is in absolute control and takes orders from no one," Rostron said. "I have never known it in our company or any other big company when a director or a managing owner would issue orders on that ship. It matters not who comes on board that ship, they are either passengers or crew. There is no official status and no authority whatever with them."

Ismay exhaled in relief.

Smith had wasted no time in calling forward his most prominent witnesses, but the hearings were far from over. Over 18 days—first in New York and then in Washington, D.C.—Smith and his colleagues interviewed surviving crew members and passengers, crew members from surrounding ships, and experts on radio communication and icebergs. All told, the committee collected over 1,100 pages of testimony from more than 80 witnesses.

Starting in May, once British survivors of the wreck had returned home, the British Wreck Commissioner conducted an inquiry of its

SAFE AT SHORE
Masses of reporters and onlookers greeted the Carpathia *when it arrived bearing the shipwreck's survivors.*

UNDER FIRE
J. Bruce Ismay (center, with mustache) took heat for his role in the crisis, fairly or not.

own. While the English press aggressively ridiculed Smith for having the audacity to keep British citizens in the United States for questioning, the two investigations largely shared the same methods and goals. The British inquiry took on an even broader scope, drawing testimonies from more than 100 witnesses over the course of 42 days.

Each investigation published a final report upon its completion, and together their recommendations had the effect of creating several significant changes in maritime safety policy that remain in place today.

✿ The International Ice Patrol was formed to identify and track icebergs that could pose danger to traveling ships. The Ice Patrol first operated as boats; today its work is done entirely in aircrafts.

✿ Passed by the U.S. government, the Radio Act of 1912 mandated that passenger ships operate their radio communication systems 24 hours a day and required nearby ships to communicate with one another, as well as with land-based radio operators.

✿ Following a conference in London, the International Convention for the Safety of Life at Sea treaty signed in January 1914 established a number of new protocols for safety at sea. Among those most relevant to the *Titanic* included a requirement that ships have enough lifeboats for every single passenger, and a standard that red rockets fired from a ship must be interpreted as a distress signal.

The work that Sen. William Alden Smith began of investigating what went wrong on the *Titanic* is a task that continues to this day. But while many mysteries remain, the earth-shaking significance of the tragedy was never in question.

"The calamity through which we have just passed has left traces of sorrow everywhere," Smith told the Senate when presenting his committee's report in late May. "Hearts have been broken and deep anguish unexpressed; art will typify with master hand its lavish contribution to the sea; soldiers of state and masters of trade will receive the homage which is their honest due; hills will be cleft in search of marble white enough to symbolize these heroic deeds, and, where kinship is the only tie that binds the lowly to the humble home bereft of son or mother or father, little groups of kinsfolk will recount, around the kitchen fire, the traits of human sympathy in those who went down with the ship." ✳

⬆ The Senate hearings took place in both New York and Washington, D.C., with 18 days of hearings in a month. More than 80 witnesses offered their testimonies.

BREAK UP
The Titanic wreckage lies in two main pieces that are about a third of a mile apart on the sea floor.

THE
RECOVERY
EFFORT

WORK TO LOCATE AND RETRIEVE THE SHIP BEGAN NOT LONG AFTER IT SANK, BUT DIDN'T BEAR FRUIT UNTIL SEVEN DECADES LATER.

The sinking of the *Titanic* has inspired treasure hunters and salvage attempts from the very beginning, but initial efforts were hampered by primitive technology and more than a few crackpot ideas (one man wanted to raise it by sending a magnetized submarine down to the sea floor). After the outbreak of World War I, interest in the wreck waned, and it seemed that people had forgotten about the disaster—until the 1950s, when *Titanic* (1953), a Hollywood film starring Clifton Webb and Barbara Stanwyck, and Walter Lord's influential book *A Night to Remember* (1955), renewed the public's interest.

The salvage proposals of the 1960s and early 1970s were just as unwieldy

> ## "I JUST STARTED TO CRY, THINKING ABOUT THE DIVE AND EVERYTHING I'D SEEN. THAT'S THE MOMENT MY TECHNICAL GUARD GOT LET DOWN AND I GOT KIND OF OVERWHELMED BY IT."
>
> *- James Cameron -*
> TITANIC DIRECTOR, ON VISITING THE WRECK

as some of their predecessors. One man wanted to attach nylon balloons to her hull, while others suggested pumping the wreck full of Vaseline and pingpong balls. In 1976, bestselling author Clive Cussler published *Raise the Titanic!*, a novel in which the ship is raised by patching its holes and filling it with compressed air. Not long afterward, real-life explorations were launched by Jack Grimm, a Texas oilman who had previously sponsored trips to find Noah's Ark, the Loch Ness Monster and a giant hole that supposedly existed in the North Pole. Though Grimm took a distinctly unscientific approach (he believed he'd found a monkey who could locate the wreck), one of his expeditions came within a mile and

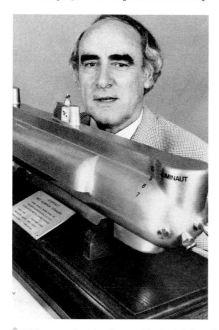

↑ While an exploration financed by Jack Grimm (left) to find the ship failed, oceanographer Robert Ballard (center) was finally successful. The contents were later revealed on a TV special hosted by Telly Savalas (right).

a half of the wreck's location. In the end, he failed to find it.

Just as it seemed that the sea had claimed the *Titanic* forever, Robert Ballard, an oceanographer from the Woods Hole Oceanographic Institution, made his first attempt to find the wreck in 1977. In September 1985, he finally located it, 370 miles off the southern coast of Newfoundland and 12,500 feet below the surface of the Atlantic Ocean. (The discovery was later revealed to be part of a secret U.S. Cold War search for two sunken nuclear submarines, the USS *Scorpion* and the USS *Thresher*.) Between 1986 and 1998, further expeditions allowed Ballard and his team to explore the wreck up close for the first time.

Ballard's 1986 expedition gave filmmaker James Cameron (then best known for the *Terminator* franchise) the idea for a new movie, one that would go on to become one of the biggest film successes of all time. In 1995, Cameron filmed his own trip to the sunken ship and used the footage in *Titanic*, his 1997 blockbuster.

In August 1998, a portion of the *Titanic* saw the light of day for the first time in over 80 years when salvage divers raised the so-called Big Piece—a 15-ton section of the liner's hull—from its watery grave. After being stored in a Santa Fe, New Mexico, laboratory for two years, it was finally put on display at the Luxor Las Vegas—a move that incited controversy. Some felt that salvaging the wreck's artifacts was

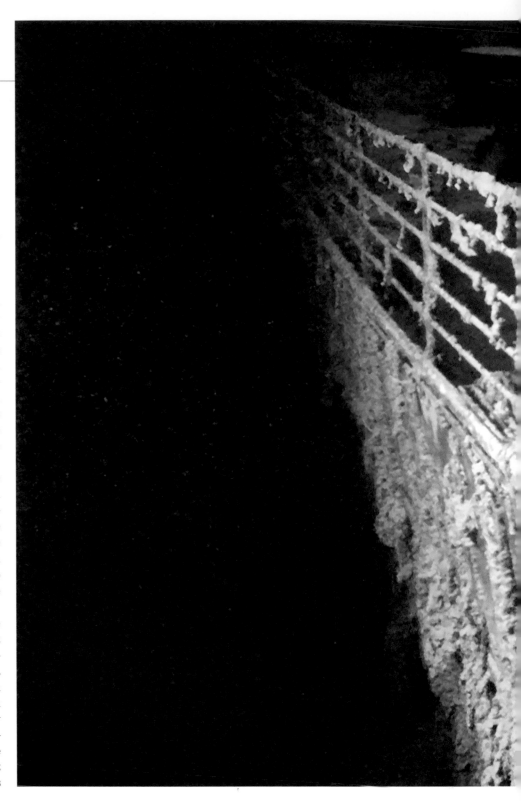

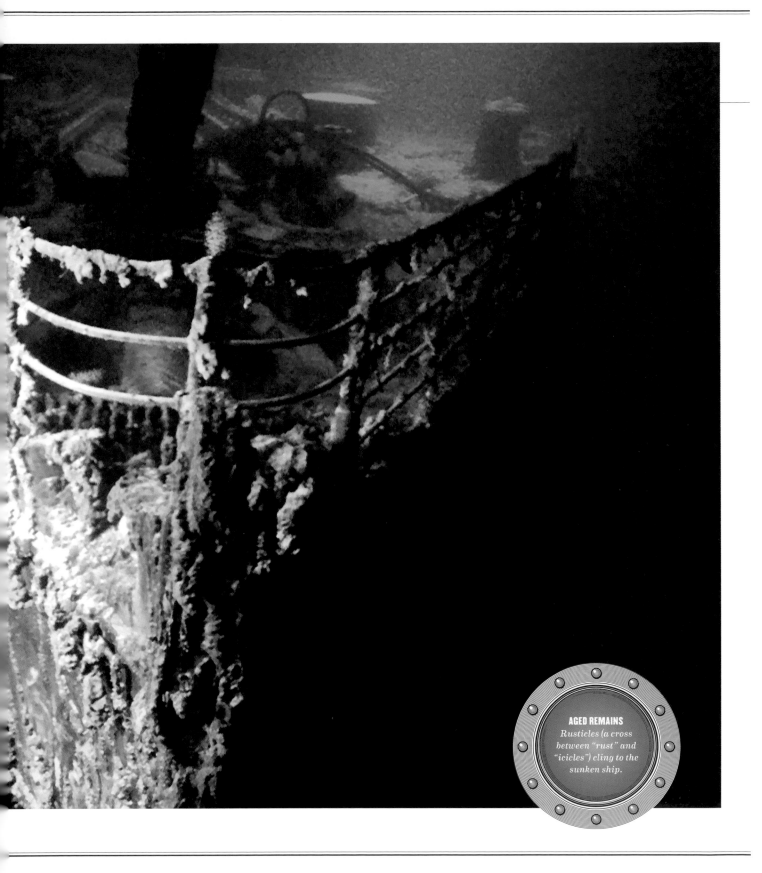

AGED REMAINS
Rusticles (a cross between "rust" and "icicles") cling to the sunken ship.

↑ "Grave robbers" is what *Titanic* survivor Eva Hart called people who profit from the wreck, like this exhibit of artifacts at the Luxor hotel in Las Vegas (above and left).

tantamount to grave robbery—and crass commercialism. (In 1987, a two-hour TV special, *Return to the Titanic Live*, had featured Telly Savalas revealing the contents of a salvaged safe.)

In May 2020, the controversy was revived when a federal ruling gave the salvage company RMS Titanic permission to retrieve the ship's Marconi telegraph—despite the protestations of lawyers from the National Oceanic and Atmospheric Administration, who argued that the machine was surrounded "by the mortal remains of more than 1,500 people."

But the salvage efforts have also been seen by some as essential acts of historic preservation, since the ship's remains are rapidly disintegrating—thanks to a combination of deep-sea currents, the saline content of the water and iron-eating bacteria that create the stalactite-like structures which have formed on the ruins. In 2019, the first photos of the wreck in 14 years showed that erosion had already caused the remains of the ship's upper levels to collapse. Some scientists estimate the *Titanic* has only about 20 years before it disintegrates entirely and is fully reclaimed by the sea. *

→ Director James Cameron used his own experiences exploring the wreck to create his groundbreaking film. Here he's shown on the set of the flooded first-class dining saloon.

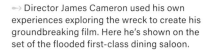

DEEP CINEMA
Cameron used a Mir submersible to film the wreck of the Titanic *for the big screen.*

Five Other Famous Shipwrecks

1 The *Mary Rose*

Launched in 1511, the *Mary Rose* was a Tudor warship that sank near the Isle of Wight off the southern coast of England during a battle with the French in 1545. It was rediscovered in 1971, but wasn't salvaged until about 10 years later—complete with thousands of artifacts and the remains of about half of the crew members, many of whom had been suffering from such ailments as arthritis and scurvy. The ship is now on display at the Mary Rose Museum in Portsmouth, England.

2 The RMS *Lusitania*

Built by the Cunard Line, the *Lusitania* was launched in 1906—one of the fastest ships of its time. (The White Star Line built the *Titanic* partly to compete with it.) On May 7, 1915, the *Lusitania* sank after being torpedoed by a German U-boat. Of the 1,959 souls aboard, only about 760 were saved. Though many objects were recovered from the wreck, it remains underwater about 11 miles south of Kinsale, Ireland.

3 The USS *Indianapolis*

Made famous by Captain Quint's haunting monologue in Steven Spielberg's *Jaws*, the USS *Indianapolis* was launched in 1931. In July 1945, the ship delivered parts of the nuclear bomb that was later dropped on Hiroshima on a top-secret mission to a U.S. Army base on Tinian, one of the Northern Mariana Islands. Afterward, the vessel was heading to the Philippines for a training mission when it was torpedoed by a Japanese submarine. It sank in 12 minutes. Of the ship's 1,195 crewmen, about 890 survived, but they suffered from exposure, dehydration and shark attacks. Only 316 were still alive when they were found four days later. In August 2017, the wreckage was discovered 5,000 feet below the surface of the Philippine Sea, where it remains to this day.

4 The *Queen Anne's Revenge*

The *Queen Anne's Revenge* was a French slave ship that was captured by the infamous pirate Edward Teach, better known as Blackbeard, near Martinique in 1717. Although he accomplished some of his most dastardly deeds on the ship, he had it for less than a year before running it aground near Beaufort, North Carolina. Its remains were discovered in 1996 and have since yielded more than 250,000 artifacts, though the ship itself still sits on the seafloor. It is now listed on the U.S. National Register of Historic Places.

5 The MV *Doña Paz*

Just before midnight on Dec. 20, 1987, the MV *Doña Paz*—a ferry carrying an estimated 4,386 passengers—was on its way from the island of Leyte to Manila, the capital of the Philippines, when it collided with the oil tanker MT *Vector*. The resulting fire engulfed both ships and spread across the oil-slicked ocean, so that most of the people who jumped overboard were incinerated or boiled. Now known as "Asia's *Titanic*," the MV *Doña Paz* was destroyed, and only 24 people survived the worst maritime disaster in Asian history.

↑ Although much of the *Mary Rose* was raised in 1982, some of the ship remains in the seabed.

CHAPMAN'S WATCH
It supposedly stopped ticking at 1:45 a.m., but the time was likely adjusted over the years.

WHAT OUTLASTED THE WRECK

*FROM A MYSTERIOUS BRACELET TO WALLETS, SHOES AND KEYS,
THESE ARE A FEW OF THE ITEMS SCAVENGED FROM THE SEABED
DECADES AFTER THE TITANIC WENT UNDER.*

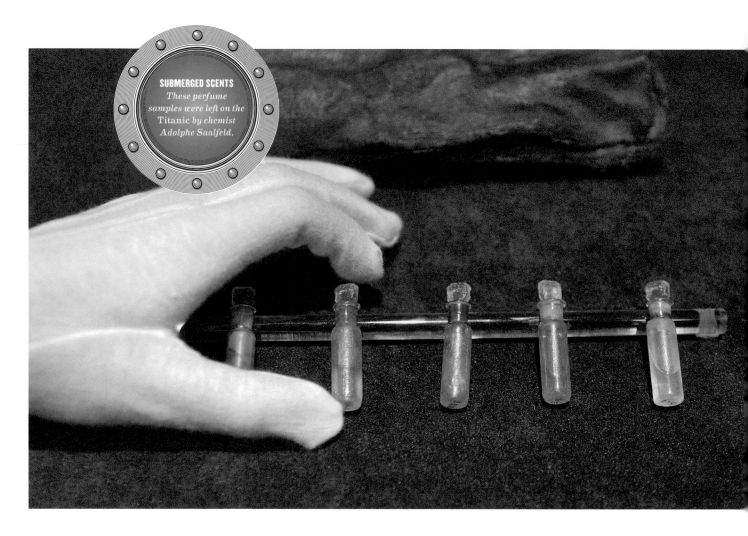

SUBMERGED SCENTS
These perfume samples were left on the Titanic by chemist Adolphe Saalfeld.

Although the bodies of the passengers who died on board the *Titanic* had entirely decomposed by the 1940s, some of the items that went down with the ship—including the shoes that sat where the bodies landed—have survived over the decades. A number of these artifacts were retrieved during the salvage missions that followed the discovery of the wreck in 1985. Here are some of the most important.

ADOLPHE SAALFELD'S PERFUME SAMPLES

The German-born Saalfeld was heading to New York as a first-class passenger on the *Titanic* with hopes of making it big in the perfume business. Although he survived the wreck, he left his samples—about 20 vials of oil—behind in a leather pouch. In 2000, the pouch was recovered in a salvage mission. "We didn't know what we discovered until we hit the surface," said Dik Barton of RMS Titanic Inc., the company that holds the rights to the ship's wreckage. "But we knew this was special immediately when we took

The mysterious "Amy" bracelet sold at auction in 2012 for an incredible $200 million.

the pouch from the collection basket and brought it to the laboratory on the ship.... A scent filled the entire lab with Edwardian perfume."

THE "AMY" BRACELET

Recovered in 1987, this bracelet features the name "Amy" spelled out in diamonds. Given its uniqueness, it's strange that no one knows for sure who it belonged to. There were two known Amys aboard the *Titanic*, but one was a crew member and the other was a third-class passenger, making it unlikely that either of them owned the valuable piece. The bracelet was found in a satchel that also contained American paper money, a diamond-tipped gold pendant inscribed "May This Be Your Lucky Star," and a case bearing the initials "R.L.B." The only person on the ship with those initials was first-class passenger Richard L. Beckwith, but his descendants have no idea who Amy was—or even if the items belonged to Beckwith. Some speculate that the items were part of a stash collected by a thief who died in the sinking.

THE WARNING BELL

Recovered in the 1985 salvage expedition, this bell was rung three times by lookout Frederick Fleet in the crow's nest of the *Titanic* in an attempt to warn the crew of the iceberg that stood in the ship's path. It is currently on display at the Titanic Historical Society in Indian Orchard, Massachusetts.

SOUND THE ALARM
Lookout Frederick Fleet rang the bell from the crow's nest in a last-ditch attempt to avoid the iceberg.

↥ Edmund Stone's effects sit on the mortuary bag that preserved them.

EDMUND STONE'S KEY AND POCKET WATCH

Used to unlock the door of a stairwell that the crew used to unload mail, the key belonged to Stone, a first-class bedroom steward who was trying to salvage hundreds of mailbags—some already soaked with seawater—from the post office and mail room as the ship sank. All of the bags were lost.

Stone, who died in the sinking, also left behind a pocket watch that stopped ticking at 2:16 a.m.—probably when he entered the water. In 2008, the watch sold at auction for $157,000.

UNKNOWN CHILD'S SHOES

Belonging to the so-called "Unknown Child"—who was later identified as 19-month-old third-class passenger

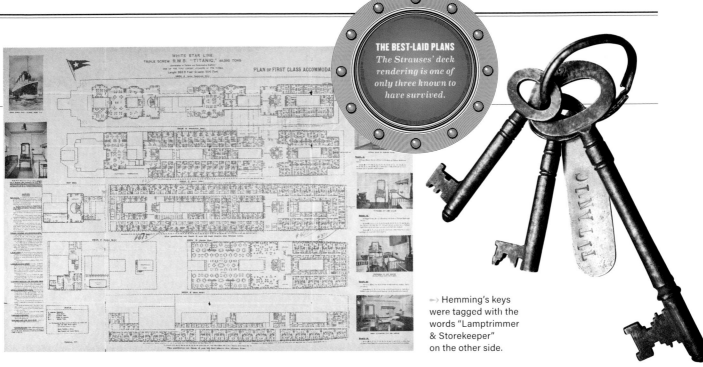

→ Hemming's keys were tagged with the words "Lamptrimmer & Storekeeper" on the other side.

Sidney Leslie Goodwin—this pair of leather shoes was found on the body of a blond boy who was retrieved by the crew of the *Mackay-Bennett*, a salvage ship that recovered bodies and belongings after the sinking. The sailors paid for a monument to the boy and placed a copper pendant in his coffin, reading "Our Babe." The boy was interred at Fairview Lawn Cemetery in Halifax, Nova Scotia, along with more than 100 of the *Titanic*'s victims. (For more on the Unknown Child, see page 132.)

MABEL BENNETT'S BEAVER COAT

One of the few pieces of clothing that survived the *Titanic* intact, this coat was worn by Bennett, a first-class stewardess, on the night of the tragedy. In the 1960s, she gave it to her great-niece, who sold it at auction for about $220,000 in 2017. It was accompanied by a note: "This coat

← These shoes were found on the body of the Unknown Child, who went for decades without being properly identified.

was worn by my Great Aunt Mabel who was a Stewardess. On her rescue from the *Titanic* she was in her nightdress and this coat was the first garment she snatched for warmth. My aunt gave me the coat…. Because of her advancing years, she found the weight of the coat too much for her."

THE SHIP'S DECK PLAN

One of the most important pieces of *Titanic* memorabilia, it belonged to Isidor and Ida Straus—the co-owner of Macy's department store and his wife—and was later used to investigate the sinking. It was rescued from the wreck by Ida's maid, Ellen Bird, and was in private hands until 2011, when it sold at auction for approximately $37,000.

ARTHUR PEUCHEN'S WALLET

Preserved because the tannin used in the process of curing leather repelled devouring sea organisms, this wallet was retrieved from the ocean floor in 1987. It contained a few business cards

and tickets for street cars in Toronto, Canada, where Peuchen lived. It was sold at auction in 2012 for an undisclosed amount.

SAMUEL HEMMING'S KEYS

Thirty minutes before the *Titanic* sank, Captain Edward Smith told Hemming, the ship's lamp trimmer, to retrieve the oil lamps from the bowels of the ship's third-class section. The lanterns were designed to help lifeboat passengers see in the dark and, more importantly, to make the lifeboats visible to rescue ships. Hemming used these brass keys to make five trips to and from the storage area, carrying four lanterns at a time, before he entered the ocean. He survived after swimming to one of the collapsible boats. In 2016, the keys were sold at auction for $26,000.

LADY DUFF-GORDON'S KIMONO

Duff-Gordon "made her escape in a very charming lavender bath robe, very beautifully embroidered, together

⟶ Madeleine Astor's life jacket. "It makes it all much more real than it has ever been," said relative Victor Astor on first seeing it.

with a very pretty blue veil," according to Edith Rosenbaum, a reporter for *Women's Wear Daily,* who was also on the *Titanic.* Known professionally as "Lucile," Duff-Gordon was one of the most influential fashion designers of the era. She almost single-handedly created the notion of upscale lingerie, making women's undergarments both fancy and risqué. The kimono she was wearing on the night of the sinking has been controversial, passing from person to person and incurring the anger of Duff-Gordon's family; they have vacillated between claiming that the kimono isn't really Duff-Gordon's and trying to get it back.

After being displayed, these gloves were put in a conservation facility in 2016.

MADELEINE ASTOR'S LIFE JACKET

On display at the Titanic Historical Society, it belonged to the wife of the ship's richest man, John Jacob Astor IV. She left it on the *Carpathia* rescue ship after she removed it in the office of a doctor's assistant.

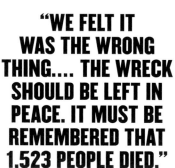

> ## "WE FELT IT WAS THE WRONG THING.... THE WRECK SHOULD BE LEFT IN PEACE. IT MUST BE REMEMBERED THAT 1,523 PEOPLE DIED."
>
> *- Margaret Meehan -*
> NIECE OF SURVIVOR VIOLET JESSOP, ON ONGOING SALVAGE EFFORTS

THE CHERUB STATUE

The grand staircase in first class was arguably the ship's most lavish and celebrated architectural element. At its base was a bronze statue of a cherub holding an illuminated torch. The statue was recovered in 1985, but was missing its lamp and left foot—possibly because it was torn from its post by a passenger who clutched it as the ship sank. Part of the railing was later found floating in the Atlantic.

WALLACE HARTLEY'S VIOLIN

The violin that Hartley, the *Titanic*'s bandleader, played with his fellow musicians as the ship sank sold at auction for $1.7 million in 2013. It was reportedly recovered inside a music case marked with his initials when Hartley's body was recovered just after the sinking.

WHITE COTTON GLOVES

No one knows who owned these gloves, but they are significant because most of the items that survived the wreck were made primarily of metal or glass. "The paper or textile items that were recovered survived because they were inside suitcases," according to Alexandra Klingelhofer, vice president of collections for Premier Exhibitions Inc. "The tanned leather of the suitcases tended to protect them [from damage in the water]."

JOHN CHAPMAN'S POCKET WATCH

The watch, belonging to second-class passenger Chapman, allegedly stopped at 1:45 a.m.—presumably when Chapman entered the waters of the North Atlantic. He was traveling on a belated honeymoon with his new bride, Lizzie, who reportedly refused to enter one of the lifeboats without her husband. "Goodbye Mrs. Richards," she told her friend Emily Richards. "If John can't go, I won't go either." The couple's story inspired characters in the 1958 film *A Night to Remember.*

SINAI KANTOR'S POCKET WATCH

Belonging to a Russian-Jewish immigrant who traveled on the *Titanic* with his wife, Miriam, it features numbers in Hebrew on its face and an image of Moses holding the Ten Commandments on the back. Sinai died in the tragedy; Miriam survived. In 2018, the watch sold at auction for $57,500. *

Lost Forever?

These priceless items reportedly went down with the **Titanic** *and will probably never be recovered.*

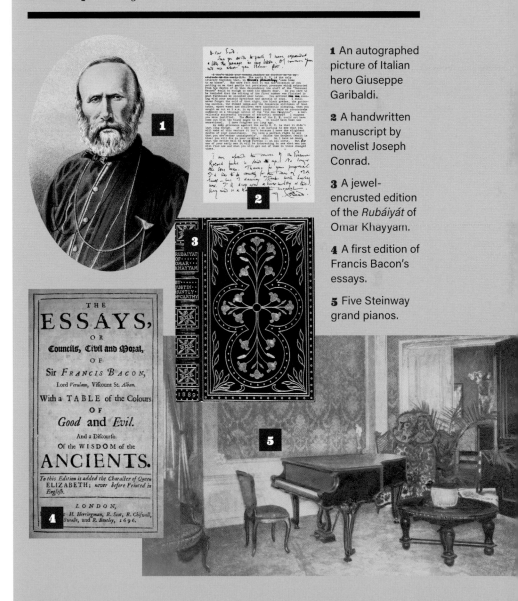

1 An autographed picture of Italian hero Giuseppe Garibaldi.

2 A handwritten manuscript by novelist Joseph Conrad.

3 A jewel-encrusted edition of the *Rubáiyát* of Omar Khayyam.

4 A first edition of Francis Bacon's essays.

5 Five Steinway grand pianos.

THE LINER'S LEGACY
"If it hadn't been for the ship going down, I'd be an American," Dean said.

THE LAST SURVIVOR'S STORY

MILLVINA DEAN WAS THE TITANIC'S FINAL LIVING SOUL.

↑ For decades after the sinking, Dean kept quiet about her part in the tragedy. But, "after they found the wreck, they found me," she said in an interview in her nursing home before she died.

"SHE KNEW HER PLACE IN HISTORY AND WAS ALWAYS WILLING TO SHARE HER STORY WITH OTHERS.... SHE WAS THE LAST LIVING LINK TO THE STORY."

- Charles Haas -

PRESIDENT OF THE
TITANIC INTERNATIONAL SOCIETY

Elizabeth Gladys "Millvina" Dean was only 2 months old when her father, 25-year-old Bertram, decided to leave England to open a tobacco shop in Wichita, Kansas. He booked transatlantic passage for himself, his wife, their 2-year-old son and Millvina, but when their first ship was grounded by the British coal strike, he bought third-class accommodations on the *Titanic*. As steerage passengers, the Deans were on the lower decks on the night of April 14 and therefore particularly aware of the impact when the ship struck the iceberg. (Many first- and second-class passengers felt little or nothing.) After going to investigate, Bertram returned to the cabin and told his wife to dress the children and head for the boat deck.

Boarding Lifeboat 10, Millvina, her mother and brother were among the first third-class passengers to leave the ship. Bertram died in the sinking (his body was never found). Along with other survivors, the Deans were brought to New York on the *Carpathia*, but their dreams of a new life in America were dashed—how could a widowed mother of two run a tobacco shop in Kansas? After spending two weeks in a hospital in New York, the Deans returned to England on the *Adriatic*. According to a contemporary account in the *Daily Mirror*, Millvina "was the pet of the liner during the voyage, and so keen was the rivalry between women to nurse this lovable mite of humanity that one of the officers decreed that first- and second-class passengers might

hold her in turn for no more than 10 minutes."

In the decades that followed the accident, Millvina and her brother used the money they received from the Titanic Relief Fund to finance their educations, but she didn't learn that she'd been aboard the doomed ship until she was 8 years old. Never married, she drew maps for the British government during World War II and later worked for an engineering company. She retired in 1972. Ironically, her brother died on April 14, 1992—exactly 80 years after the *Titanic* struck its fatal iceberg.

Though Millvina initially resisted being publicly associated with the *Titanic*, she eventually became a regular participant in memorials and conventions, giving interviews and

⇡ Millvina at age 3 with her mother, older brother and dog. "I believe in fate because we weren't supposed to go on the *Titanic* at all," she said.

appearing in documentaries—particularly after Robert Ballard and his team discovered the sunken ship. "Until the wreckage of the *Titanic* was found in 1985, nobody was interested in me," she said. "Who expects to become famous at that age?" On Oct. 16, 2007, she became the last living survivor of the tragedy when Barbara West Dainton died at age 96.

Millvina lived in Ashurst, a village in Hampshire, England, until infirmities forced her into a nearby nursing home. Toward the end of her life, unable to afford her room, she sold her priceless keepsakes—including a suitcase filled with clothes that were given to the Deans when they arrived in New York. But the mementos that sold at auction were eventually returned to her by the buyer. Around the same time, Leonardo DiCaprio and Kate Winslet, the stars of the 1997 blockbuster *Titanic*, along with the film's director, James Cameron, donated £20,000 (about $25,000) to the Millvina Fund, established to pay for her care bills. (Knowing that her father had died on the ship, Millvina refused to see the movie.)

After Millvina died of pneumonia in 2009, her ashes were scattered off the docks in Southampton, where she and her family had embarked on their fateful voyage nearly a century before. *

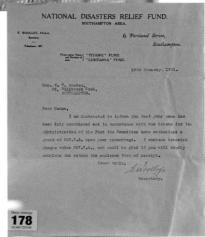

↑ Some of the *Titanic* memorabilia that Dean was forced to sell was later returned to her—including a suitcase and letters from the Titanic Relief Fund.

The Tragedies After the Tragedy

These four survivors never quite escaped the Titanic.

Jack Thayer

A 17-year-old first-class passenger, Thayer escaped the sinking of the *Titanic* by jumping off the deck. Braving the frigid water, he managed to swim to Collapsible Lifeboat B, which had overturned after being swept off the sinking ship. He and several other survivors managed to keep the vessel afloat until they were rescued by Lifeboat 12. They were eventually brought to the *Carpathia*, where Thayer reunited with his mother. His father drowned in the Atlantic.

In 1943, after his son Edward was shot down in the Pacific during World War II, Thayer was overcome by a depression that worsened after his mother died on April 14, 1944—the 32nd anniversary of the *Titanic* sinking. The following year, Thayer was found dead with his throat and wrists slashed in his car parked in a West Philadelphia lot. The verdict was suicide.

While it's hard for anyone to bear the deaths of loved ones, and Thayer probably inherited a tendency toward depression from his father, he clearly remained haunted by the *Titanic*. "It seems to me that the disaster...was the event that not only made the world rub its eyes and awake but woke it with a start keeping it moving at a rapidly accelerating pace...with less and less peace, satisfaction and happiness," he later wrote. "To my mind the world of today awoke April 15th, 1912."

Constance Willard

"It was like waiting to get a chance at the cloak room of a crowded opera house," 20-year-old Willard, a first-class passenger, said of the disaster. After she returned to her native Duluth, Minnesota, Willard began to show symptoms of what we now call post-traumatic stress disorder (PTSD). She thought that the disaster had happened "ages ago" but always felt "sort of an apathy.... I have a kind of a 'don't care what happens' feeling."

Later, Willard descended into full-blown mental illness and was hospitalized at Las Campanas Hospital in Compton, California. Her hair had gone completely white, and one staff member called her "prematurely aged." She never mentioned the *Titanic*. One night, the hospital screened *A Night to Remember*, the 1958 British film about the ship's last night, for its patients. Willard sat and watched with no discernible reaction. She died at age 73.

Annie Robinson

A 40-year-old stewardess, Robinson escaped aboard Lifeboat 11 at 1:40 a.m., but was plagued by flashbacks. On Oct. 9, 1914, she was sailing across the Atlantic on the steamer *Devonian* to visit relatives in Boston when the ship entered thick fog. The ship's officers later said that she was in "a high state of excitement because of the fog and the sounding of the fog horn," *The New York Times* reported. Convinced that another disaster was imminent, she jumped overboard. Her body was never found.

Charles Stengel

First-class passenger Stengel was moaning in his sleep aboard the *Titanic* when his wife, Annie, woke him. "You're dreaming," she said. Moments later, they heard the crash. Annie escaped in Lifeboat 5, not knowing the pair would be reunited. "The nearest thing I've ever known to heaven on Earth was meeting my husband again on the deck of the *Carpathia*," she said. But just five days after the disaster, Charles died suddenly at the Stengels' home in Newark, New Jersey. Though the cause of death was not officially determined, his physicians chalked it up to "delayed shock."

SMALL TREASURE
Tucked away for years, the Unknown Child's shoes were eventually donated to the Maritime Museum of the Atlantic.

THE UNKNOWN CHILD

NEARLY A CENTURY AFTER THE SHIPWRECK, RESEARCHERS FINALLY SOLVED ONE OF THE TITANIC'S MOST PUZZLING MYSTERIES.

On the afternoon of Wednesday, April 17, 1912—approximately 36 hours after the sinking of the *Titanic*—the CS *Mackay-Bennett* left port from Halifax, Nova Scotia. It was the first ship contracted by White Star Line to recover bodies from the wreck. Carrying embalming supplies, 100 coffins and over 100 tons of ice for the preservation of corpses, the *Mackay-Bennett* traveled four days through fog and choppy waters to reach the site of the *Titanic*'s sinking.

Once on the scene, it became clear that the ship would not be able to accommodate all of the bodies discovered by its crew. For one thing, there wasn't enough room. But the greater limiting factor was a lack of sufficient embalming supplies. The ship only had enough for a few dozen bodies, and it was against maritime law to reenter port with unembalmed corpses.

What commenced was a class-based selection system, one far more stark and grim than the system that divided passengers when they were alive. The bodies of first-class passengers were embalmed and stored in coffins, while second-class passengers were embalmed and wrapped in canvas. Fifty-one corpses returned to Halifax on the *Mackay-Bennett*, and 116 passengers were buried at sea—all third-class passengers.

There was, however, one exception. Twenty-four-year-old Cliff Crease was a crewman out on lifeboats collecting bodies. His diary entry from his first day out on the water tells the

ON THE SCENE
Halifax was the closest major port to the site of the disaster, and the base of the CS Mackay-Bennett recovery ship.

story of the day's events in a matter-of-fact way:

Fine weather. Started to pick up bodies at six a.m. and continued 'til five thirty p.m. Recovered fifty-one bodies, forty-six-men and one baby.... Bodies in good state but badly bruised by being knocked about in the water.

While the diary gives a purely factual account, hauling the lifeless bodies out of the freezing Atlantic was undoubtedly a harrowing experience. The baby Crease mentions in his diary entry was the fourth body pulled from the water, recovered by Crease himself. It was a moment he'd never forget.

"He never fully recovered," Crease's granddaughter Rabia Wilcox said years later. "He told our father it was the worst thing that ever happened to him."

The coroner's description of the young child's body provided a straightforward account of the boy's appearance. It read:

No. 4. - MALE. - ESTIMATED AGE, 2. - HAIR, FAIR.
CLOTHING - Grey coat with fur on collar and cuffs; brown serge frock; petticoat; flannel garment; pink woolen singlet – brown shoes and stockings.
NO MARKS WHATEVER
PROBABLY THIRD CLASS

While only the bodies of the first- and second-class passengers were drawn from the waters, Crease and the rest of the crew felt a special connection to the child, and felt they must bring his body back to shore.

Back in Halifax, a well-attended funeral was held for the boy at St. George's Anglican Church on May 4. And just as it had moved the crewmen of the *Mackay-Bennett*, the story of the unidentified infant resonated with the people of Nova Scotia. A number of local families volunteered to sponsor the service and burial. But it was Cliff Crease, Captain F.H. Lardner and the rest of the crew

of the *Mackay-Bennett* who were ultimately granted the duties of burying the child.

After the funeral, six of the ship's crew carried the boy's white casket out of St. George's. He was buried at nearby Fairview Cemetery, in a section specially arranged for victims of the *Titanic* disaster. While his family was unknown, the sailors left him with a token of their kinship, a medallion inscribed, "Our Babe." The child's black marble gravestone read:

Erected to the Memory of an Unknown Child Whose Remains Were Recovered after the Disaster of the Titanic, *April 15, 1912*

In the decades following, the grave remained something of a sacred site for Halifax locals, and also an attraction for *Titanic* historians and enthusiasts. Per his gravestone, the boy became known as the Unknown Child. One common belief held that he was Gösta Pålsson, son of Alma Pålsson. Alma had brought all four of her children aboard the *Titanic* as she voyaged from Sweden to Chicago. Like Gösta, the Unknown Child was 2 years old when he passed away, with the same fair hair. Plus, Alma's grave was right behind the boy's in Fairview. Could fate have placed mother and son side by side in death?

But it was merely a theory, and there was little thought that the mystery of the child's identity would ever be solved. After all, what new evidence is there to be uncovered years after a shipwreck?

NO. 4 - MALE - ESTIMATED AGE, 2 - HAIR, FAIR

CLOTHING - Grey coat with fur on collar and cuffs; brown serge frock; petticoat; flannel garment; pink woolen singlet - brown shoes and stockings.

NO MARKS WHATEVER

PROBABLY THIRD CLASS

As it turned out, plenty.

In 1999, Ryan Parr of the Paleo-DNA Laboratory at Ontario's Lakehead University stumbled upon a TV show about the *Titanic*'s unidentified victims. At the time, his most recent project had been identifying historical familial relationships through DNA analysis at an ancient Egyptian cemetery. It occurred to him that the same methods might be able to solve some of the *Titanic*'s mysteries.

"I thought 'Wow, I wonder if anyone is interested or still cares about the unidentified victims of the *Titanic*?'" he recalled years later.

Parr connected with Alan Ruffman, a geologist also interested in discovering the identities of passengers buried in Fairview Cemetery. After securing permission to exhume several bodies at the cemetery, they prepared to dig up the corpses in 2001. On the first day, they were met with a local who had chained himself to the grave of the Unknown Child, declaring himself the boy's spiritual guardian. However, once convinced that the researchers' intent was noble, he abruptly unchained himself and left.

In most of the graves, Parr and Ruffman and their team were unable to find usable samples. But in the Unknown Child's, which sat on higher ground than the others, they were able to recover three teeth and 6 centimeters of arm bone. While not a guarantee of success, it was an excellent starting point for Parr's molecular-level studies.

The team began their search for DNA matches with the most obvious candidates: the Pålsson family. Parr's particular method of DNA analysis involved mitochondrial DNA (mtDNA), a type of DNA shared among members of the same maternal ancestral line. They were able to track down maternal ancestors of Alma and Gösta Pålsson in Sweden, but the mtDNA samples did not match those from the Unknown Child.

Thanks to worldwide collaboration among historians, genealogists, translators and ancestors of passengers, the researchers finally narrowed their list to two candidates: 13-month-old Eino Viljami Panula of Finland and 19-month-old Sidney Leslie Goodwin of England. Incredibly, mtDNA samples from ancestors of both young boys matched that of the Unknown Child, suggesting that the two were distant cousins. The tiebreaker was the teeth, deemed by experts to have belonged to a child between 9 and 15 months old. Researchers made the results public: the Unknown Child was finally known, and it was Eino Viljami Panula.

Or was it? The dental analysis was based on an estimate, and Goodwin wasn't far removed from that 9-to-15-months range at 19 months old. Plus, the recovered teeth were degraded from nearly a century of decomposition, meaning those estimates may have been imprecise. Work continued on the case.

Game-changing evidence arrived in 2002 when Earle Northover donated a pair of brown shoes to the Nova Scotia Museum. The shoes, he said, had been

"[THE RECOVERY CREW WAS] MOVED WHEN THEY SAW... WHAT LOOKED LIKE A BUNDLE OF CLOTHING FLOATING IN THE WATER AND TURNED OUT TO BE THIS...BOY."

- Blair Beed -

AUTHOR, *TITANIC VICTIMS IN HALIFAX GRAVEYARDS*

in the possession of his grandfather, Clarence Northover, who had been a Halifax police sergeant in 1912.

"Clothing was burned to stop souvenir hunters, but he was too emotional when he saw the little pair of brown, leather shoes about fourteen centimeters long, and didn't have the heart to burn them," Earle Northover wrote of his grandfather in a letter to the museum. "When no relatives came to claim the shoes, he placed them in his desk drawer at the police station, and there they remained for the next six years, until he retired in 1918."

Together, several pieces of circumstantial evidence suggested that the shoes belonged to the Unknown Child, and also Sidney Leslie Goodwin. They matched the coroner's description of the brown shoes worn by the child.

They were likely made in England, Goodwin's home country, according to textile historians. And, perhaps most critically, the shoes were too large for a 13-month-old, but just the right size for a boy of 19 months.

More definitive proof soon followed. Looking at another section of mtDNA, Parr's team found evidence that suggested Goodwin was the Unknown Child. Researchers at the U.S. Armed Forces DNA Identification Laboratory in Dover, Delaware, suggested the same. Along with the emergence of the shoes, the new mtDNA evidence sealed the deal in Parr's mind.

"Luckily, it was a rare [mtDNA] difference, so that is what gives you 98% certainty the identification is correct," he said.

The full story emerged: Goodwin's entire family rode aboard the *Titanic* as third-class passengers. All eight—including his parents, Frederick and August, and five older siblings—perished in the shipwreck.

In August 2008, ancestors of the Goodwins held a memorial at Fairview Cemetery beside the grave of the once-unknown child. They were given the opportunity to change the engraving on the gravestone, but instead decided to add Sidney's name to the existing message. As relative Carol Goodwin described, the inscription was perfect as it was.

"The tombstone of the Unknown Child represents all of the children who perished on the *Titanic*, and we left it that way," she said. ✶

TO THE MEMORY
OF AN
UNKNOWN CHILD
WHOSE REMAINS
WERE RECOVERED
AFTER THE
DISASTER TO
THE "TITANIC"
APRIL 15 TH 1912

SIDNEY LESLIE
GOODWIN
SEPT. 9, 1910
APR. 15, 1912

REST IN PEACE
Visitors still come to the Unknown Child's grave marker to pay their respects to those who were lost.

TWIN PEAKS
The Olympia and Titanic were sister ships, but did the former replace the latter before the crash?

THE DARK SIDE

LIKE ANY PROMINENT DISASTER, THE WRECK OF
THE TITANIC PROVOKED A NUMBER OF CONSPIRACY THEORIES—
SOME MORE OUTLANDISH THAN OTHERS. HERE ARE A FEW.

THEORY #1: J.P. MORGAN SANK THE *TITANIC*

Having purchased White Star Line in 1902 and folded it into the International Mercantile Marine Company, it was John Pierpont Morgan whose money largely financed the construction of the *Titanic*. And as the indirect owner of the ship, one might think Morgan would want to ride on its maiden voyage. After all, many of his high-society peers had purchased tickets for the historic ride. But while he was originally scheduled to leave Southampton aboard the *Titanic* on April 10, 1912, he canceled his trip in late March and remained in Europe.

On Dec. 23, 1913—just over 20 months after the tragic shipwreck—the Federal Reserve was founded. This creation of an American central bank was a major moment in world economic history. It was also the culmination of a yearslong effort by Morgan, who had played a key role in bailing out the U.S. banking system multiple times to that point.

But was the creation of the Federal Reserve so important to Morgan that he would murder those who stood in its way—and hundreds more on top of that? That's the central thesis of this conspiracy theory, which posits that Morgan orchestrated the sinking of the *Titanic* to kill off passengers John Jacob Astor IV, Isidor Straus and Benjamin Guggenheim—all prominent opponents of the Federal Reserve.

Even beyond the fact that there is no evidence to support it, there are a number of holes in this theory. For one, the logistics of such a plot seem unworkable. Would one or several crewmen accept a bribe to wreck the ship knowing that they had no guarantee of surviving themselves? Would those hypothetical suspects even know how to intentionally wreck a ship to the point of sinking? And how would they make sure that Astor, Straus and Guggenheim wouldn't survive?

Secondly, Morgan's actual reason for canceling his ticket is well-documented. He was in Europe in the first place to ship a personal art collection housed in England and France to New York, where it would find a home at the Metropolitan Museum of Art. However, a customs issue delayed the shipment, forcing Morgan to remain in Europe until mid-April.

Lastly—and this is the real kicker —Astor, Straus and Guggenheim weren't even opponents of the Federal Reserve. An archival newspaper search by the *Washington Post* found that Astor and Guggenheim hadn't spoken out on the issue one way or another, and that Straus had in fact publicly come out in favor of the central bank multiple times.

THEORY #2: IT WAS REALLY THE *OLYMPIC*

Constructed by White Star Line in the same Belfast shipyard, the RMS *Olympic* was a true sister ship to the *Titanic*. It was finished several months earlier, and embarked on its maiden voyage in June 1911. All was

↓ The White Star Line was once one of the world's most powerful shipping lines. It merged with the Cunard Line in 1934.

MAN OF MEANS
At his peak, J.P. Morgan was worth $80 million—about $1.2 billion in today's money.

well until September when, on its fifth voyage, *Olympic* collided with HMS *Hawke* and sustained significant damage. It returned to Southampton, England, for initial maintenance, then to Belfast for more major repairs.

The financial hit to White Star Line was substantial. The collision was deemed to be the fault of the *Olympic*, so White Star had to pay up for its repairs. The company also racked up large legal costs in unsuccessful insurance claims, and lost revenue while *Olympic* was out of operation. To make matters worse, *Olympic* lost a propeller blade during a February 1912 voyage, necessitating yet another round of repairs. The various *Olympic* incidents caused White Star to delay the *Titanic*'s maiden voyage by three weeks, costing even more money.

If some theorists are to be believed, it cost them enough money to swap in the damaged *Olympic* for the bally-hooed *Titanic*, sink it and collect on the insurance to cover their losses.

It's a theory that goes back nearly as far as the incident itself. "The architect, the owner and the Captain were partners in an infamous conspiracy to repair their desperate fortunes by sinking the ship and sharing the insurance money," wrote a lawyer in a letter to the editor of London newspaper *The Times* in 1914. More recently, a series of books published during the late 1990s pushed the same theory.

While perhaps a fun conspiracy theory, it holds no weight as an actual theory of what took place. One hopes

"BUSINESS WILL DENY ME THE PLEASURE OF BEING ONE OF THE FIRST TO CROSS ON THE FINEST VESSEL OF THE IMM [INTERNATIONAL MERCANTILE MARINE]."
- *J.P. Morgan* -
CABLE REGARDING HIS CANCELLATION OF TRAVEL ABOARD THE *TITANIC*

the folks at White Star Line would value hundreds of human lives more than any amount of money, but even if they didn't, it's hard to imagine an insurance payout outweighing the hit that the company took to its reputation after the *Titanic* sank. Furthermore, the numbers don't add up. Analysis suggests that the cost of damage to the *Olympic* didn't exceed $125,000, while the *Titanic* was underinsured by $2.5 million. In other words, the elaborate switcheroo would have cost White Star far more money than it would have saved them.

THEORY #3: A FIRE STRIKES ICE

About 10 days before the *Titanic* left on its maiden voyage, a fire began in one of its coal bunkers. That fire lasted not just up until the ship's trip, but several

DIVERTING RESOURCES
When a propeller blade fell off the Olympic, the builders had to pull workers off the Titanic *to help make repairs.*

days into it. While that may sound concerning to those unfamiliar with steamships—surely a ship should not set sail while an unintentional fire takes place—such blazes were a common occurrence in coal bunkers. When well-managed, they posed no danger to the ship or its passengers.

But was the fire aboard the *Titanic* under control? Or did it play a leading role in the ship's demise?

In 2017, *Titanic: The New Evidence* aired on British television. In the documentary, Irish journalist Senan Molony points to a photograph that he claims shows the *Titanic*'s hull scarred and weakened by the blaze, primed to rupture when striking an iceberg. Molony also suggests that the shoveling of coals in engine furnaces, a common method of putting out these blazes, caused the ship to accelerate into the iceberg at an unsafe speed.

Naturally, the documentary drew interest from *Titanic* historians, most of whom took issue with Molony's theories. For starters, the alleged scar in the photograph does not appear in other images of *Titanic* from the same time, suggesting it may be a reflection or a defect. It's also 50 feet away from the location of the coal bunker fire. So even if it were a real marking, its linkage to the fire would be highly suspect.

As for whether efforts to extinguish the blaze caused *Titanic* to speed into ice? According to testimony from multiple survivors, the fire was put out for good on April 13, the day before the ship struck the iceberg. ✳

INSTANT CLASSIC
Despite running $100 million over budget and costly delays, the 1997 Titanic film was an unabashed hit.

CHAPTER 4

Legacy of the Titanic

From blockbuster movies to ongoing exhibits and permanent memorials, we continue to be fascinated by the ship, the passengers and their stories.

THE *TITANIC* AT THE MOVIES

FILMS ABOUT THE LINER RANGE FROM THE
NOTEWORTHY TO THE NOTORIOUS.

ONE FOR THE RECORDS

JAMES CAMERON'S TITANIC IS RIGHTLY REMEMBERED AS A BOX-OFFICE SMASH AND A CULTURAL PHENOMENON. BUT FOR CAMERON, CAST AND CREW, THE MOVIE-MAKING VOYAGE WAS A STRANGE AND DIFFICULT TRIP.

⬆ "The film is about death and separation; [Jack] had to die," James Cameron told *Vanity Fair* about the tear-jerking 1997 movie ending.

I n the mid '90s, not much on James Cameron's CV would suggest he was the right man to direct a romance set aboard the *Titanic*. The director's track record was impressive—and did include a deep-sea thriller with 1989's *The Abyss*— but *The Terminator* and *Aliens* weren't exactly conventional love stories.

But the idea of making a *Titanic* movie hadn't left Cameron's mind since 1987, when he watched a *National Geographic* documentary on Robert Ballard's 1985 expedition to the ship's wreckage. An outline for a project of his own immediately took shape.

"Do story with bookends of present-day scene…intercut with memory of

⇡ Already popular, the movie's blockbuster success rocketed actors Leonardo DiCaprio and Kate Winslet to super stardom.

a survivor," he scribbled in a note to himself. "Needs a mystery or driving plot element."

When Cameron first met with Fox executives in Spring 1995 to pitch his *Titanic* idea, they were taken aback.

"They were like, 'Ooooooh-kaaaaaay,'" he later said. "'A three-hour romantic epic? Sure, that's just what we want. Is there a little bit of *Terminator* in that? Any Harrier jets, shoot-outs or car chases?' I said, 'No, no, no. It's not like that.'"

The unexpected subject matter was but one eyebrow-raising component of Cameron's proposal. The director requested a massive $125 million budget; just the previous year, his feature *True Lies* had been the first film to ever top a $100 million budget. Cameron and the studio settled on $110 million, with the director sacrificing $4 million of his own salary.

With a deal in place, Cameron—along with casting director Mali Finn—set forth on finding the actors who would become his Jack and Rose. They had a tight line to walk: The roles required youth and exuberance, while the film's price tag and high profile demanded established Hollywood star power.

First suggested by Finn, Kate Winslet was more young than established. But she had starred in multiple romances before age 20, and Cameron flew her out to Los Angeles for screen tests on Finn's recommendation. After nailing a couple of screen tests, Winslet grew tired of waiting on Cameron's decision. She called the director on his car phone, reaching him as he was driving on the highway. "I *am* your Rose," she insisted. She was cast soon after.

Leonardo DiCaprio had a higher profile than Winslet, but less polish. He had made his name in cinema playing troubled young men, and the free-spirited, unburdened character of Jack Dawson did not speak to him. When paired with Winslet in the audition room, he had to be cajoled to read the role even just a single time. But that one take was enough for Cameron to know he had found his Jack.

Once production began, nothing was more important to Cameron than historical accuracy. A perfectionist, he felt he owed it to both audiences and the memories of *Titanic* passengers to deliver a flawless retelling of events. That started with a 40-acre set in Rosarito, Mexico, built at a breakneck pace over 100 days. After blasting a hole with 10,000 tons of dynamite, the construction team built a 17 million gallon tank to hold the replica ship.

And aboard that ship: a perfect recreation, or as close to perfect as possible. Dinnerware and flatware was emblazoned with the White Star Line logo, even though it would be invisible to filmgoers. When set designers proposed using paint to look like wallpaper, Cameron insisted on the

"FOR ONE SPLIT SECOND A SHAFT OF LIGHT CAME DOWN FROM THE HEAVENS AND LIT UP THE FOREST."
- James Cameron -
SPEAKING ON LEONARDO DiCAPRIO'S RELUCTANT *TITANIC* AUDITION

real thing. He spent whole days handaging furniture. When he saw a tile stain during the filming of one scene, he leaped out of his director's chair to buff it out himself. He even sketched Jack's portraits for the iconic "draw me like one of your French girls" scene.

If working under such obsessive, tireless leadership sounds exhausting, that's because it was. Overnight shoots were frequent—given how many of the film's key scenes took place in the dark—with Cameron taking his "lunch break" at 2 a.m. Each shooting of a sinking scene necessitated resetting the replica ship's ornate dining room, a gargantuan task to perform time and time again. And Cameron intensified the already brutal working conditions by shouting at his crew.

The actors got off a little easier—even Cameron knew better than to alienate his stars—but still faced a test of endurance. During in-water shoots, actors had to be monitored for signs of hypothermia. When filming in the water for prolonged periods, DiCaprio and Winslet would take turns swimming to the far side of the tank to pee. Winslet received deep bruising from the strenuous scenes, even chipping a bone in her elbow.

Furthermore, outside pressures began to breach the bubble of the set. Falling behind schedule, Cameron quickly blew past his already substantial budget. During one two-week stretch alone, the expected budget ballooned by $20 million. It would hit $200 million when all was said and done. "We were carrying the movie on our books as a $55 million loss at the time," said Peter Chernin, then head of 20th Century Fox.

One night, Fox exec Bill Mechanic visited the set with a list of proposed cuts to try and rein Cameron in.

"Jim exploded," said Mechanic. "It was 3 or 4 o'clock in the morning, and if he'd had a gun in his trailer he would have shot me. The gist of it was, 'If you're so f---ing smart, you direct the picture.' And he walked off. He stormed out of his trailer, pulled his chauffeur out of the car, and sped off."

Filming finished with Cameron still at the helm, but news of the bloated budget and three-hour-plus runtime had made the film something of a laughingstock. Fox had cut a record-breaking check on a movie that no one in their right mind would sit through.

Of course, that's not quite how things worked out. After debuting in December 1997, *Titanic* became a cultural phenomenon. It was No. 1 at the box office for 15 consecutive weeks, remaining in theaters for almost a year. It made $600 million domestically and over $2.2 billion worldwide, both records that would stand until Cameron made *Avatar* in 2009. *Titanic* was nominated for 14 Oscars and won 11, including Best Picture.

While *Titanic*'s success is remembered as a foregone conclusion, the film's popularity was never James Cameron's primary concern. He'd sought to make a movie true to the legacy of the ship and its passengers, and audiences followed.

"*Titanic* was seen as a blockbuster, interestingly enough, only after the fact, when it made a lot of money," Cameron said. "I think of *Titanic* as the biggest independent film that's ever been made, because it had that sensibility of an independent film."*

A Rose (or Jack) by Any Other Name

Leonardo DiCaprio's Jack Dawson and Kate Winslet's Rose DeWitt Bukater seemed destined to become a classic on-screen couple. But a number of Hollywood stars were considered for each role.

JACK

Christian Bale
Known for his intense method-style acting, few stars commit to a role like Bale. So one can only imagine his disappointment in being ruled out for Jack. But that hardly slowed the actor's award-winning career.

Tom Cruise
Cruise was interested in *Titanic*, but his asking price was reportedly too high. Ironically, DiCaprio supposedly made upwards of $40 million thanks to a contractual clause that gave him a small (but significant) cut of revenue.

Matthew McConaughey
McConaughey was a red-hot commodity in Tinseltown in the mid-'90s. His contention for Jack was so strong that he even read for the part with Winslet. "Walked away from there pretty confident that I had it," he later recalled.

ROSE

Claire Danes
After co-starring with DiCaprio in 1997's *Romeo + Juliet*, Danes was a natural choice. But her working relationship with Leo was actually a deterrent: "I was feeling eager to have different creative experiences and that felt like a repeat."

Gwyneth Paltrow
For years, rumors persisted that Paltrow had declined the role of Rose. In a 2015 interview with Howard Stern, Paltrow finally addressed the rumors. "I think I was really in contention for it—I was one of the last two," she said.

Many, Many More
The list of actresses considered for Rose rivaled the length of the *Titanic* itself. Among them: Drew Barrymore (above), Angelina Jolie, Winona Ryder, Jennifer Aniston, Charlize Theron, Uma Thurman, Jennifer Connelly and Madonna.

MORE CLASSIC FILMS

FROM DOCUMENTARIES TO MUSICALS, HOLLYWOOD HAS HAD NUMEROUS TAKES ON THE FATAL VOYAGE.

VANISHED HISTORY
Experts believe that the destruction of this film is one of the greatest losses in silent-film history.

Saved From The Titanic

ECLAIR'S EXCLUSIVE EXTRA
A Startling Story of the Sea's Greatest Tragedy
By Miss DOROTHY GIBSON, A Survivor
SHE IS SUPPORTED BY A POWERFUL CAST
Six Color and Gold Posters, Herald's Photos
A FILM WITHOUT A PARALLEL

| TUESDAY MAY 14 | Eclair Film Co. FORT LEE, N. J. SALES COMPANY, Sole Agents | TUESDAY MAY 14 |

SAVED FROM THE TITANIC
1912

The first film about the disaster was cowritten by the actress Dorothy Gibson, a *Titanic* survivor who starred as herself (her costume consisted of the actual dress she wore on the night of the sinking). Released less than a month after the tragedy, it was a massive success, but proved to be Gibson's undoing. Traumatized after reliving the incident on-screen, Gibson literally walked away from her career: One day, she left the studio and never came back. The film's negative was destroyed in a fire; only stills survive.

ATLANTIC 1929

The first sound film about the tragedy, it was also the first to show the ship's band playing "Nearer, My God, to Thee." The filmmakers changed the name of the doomed liner after the White Star Line threatened to sue.

TITANIC 1943

Made by the Nazis under propaganda chief Joseph Goebbels, this film depicted the ship's British officers as buffoons, blamed American capitalism for the disaster and added a fictitious German crew member as the "hero." It was the first film about the *Titanic* to put fictional characters at the center of the real-life events—later a cinematic convention.

CREEPY CREDITS
Four clips from the Nazi film were later recycled in Britain's A Night to Remember.

TITANIC 1953

This Hollywood outing starred Clifton Webb as a wealthy American expatriate in Europe who books a ticket on the *Titanic* after learning that his wife (Barbara Stanwyck) has kidnapped their two children and taken them on the ship to escape her rocky marriage. Sound far-fetched? Maybe—but it's a retelling of a similar scenario, when Michel Navratil kidnapped his two young sons, Michel Jr. and Edmond, from their mother and took them on the *Titanic*. (For more on their story, see page 36.)

A NIGHT TO REMEMBER

1958

It's been said that there were two defining moments in the creation of the *Titanic* myth: 1912, the year the ship sank, and 1955, when Walter Lord published *A Night to Remember*. Fast-paced and compulsively readable, the bestselling nonfiction book was based on interviews with survivors and almost single-handedly renewed public interest in the *Titanic*. The movie version is unsentimental, unflinching and almost like a documentary; one of the ship's survivors, Renée Harris, walked out of a screening saying it was too "realistic."

THE UNSINKABLE MOLLY BROWN

1964

Could passengers on the doomed ship possibly have imagined that their experience would become a Broadway musical less than 50 years later? Or that four years after that, it would be adapted into a film starring Debbie Reynolds as the colorful, courageous Margaret (Molly) Brown? One of the ship's best-known passengers, Brown was anything but an unsung hero—in more ways than one—but her spirit shined through the fictional retelling.

RAISE THE TITANIC

1980

Based on the bestselling novel by Clive Cussler, this fictionalized version of the wreck's recovery was released five years before the ship was actually discovered. The plot is pure bunk, focusing on Cold War shenanigans involving the CIA, nuclear war and the quest for a rare mineral that supposedly sank in the *Titanic*. Nevertheless, the special effects remain impressive.

HOLMES & WATSON

2018

This buddy comedy shows Sherlock Holmes (Will Ferrell, left) and Dr. Watson (John C. Reilly) trying to save Queen Victoria from a time bomb that is hidden in a kettle drum aboard the *Titanic*. Forget the fact that Victoria died in 1901 and the ship sailed in 1912—historical accuracy is beside the point here. Although the film features a charming cameo from Billy Zane, who had played Caledon Hockley in Cameron's 1997 *Titanic*, it is otherwise (no pun intended) a disaster. ✳

Big-Screen Bloopers

The two best films about the *Titanic* (*A Night to Remember* and 1997's *Titanic*) have been celebrated for their accuracy, but both took their share of liberties. In 1958's *Night*, the ship is christened with a bottle of Champagne on its bow, but that never happened—the scene was inserted because filmmakers thought audiences expected it. And like every film about the *Titanic* made before the wreck was discovered, *Night* shows the ship sinking intact, when in fact it broke in two—an event not reflected on film until the 1996 TV miniseries *Titanic*.

While James Cameron's *Titanic* contained the most accurate sets of any film, there are some gaffes. On Jack's way to meet Rose for dinner, a steward lets him through a door leading into the ship's grand staircase. But that door led from the deck where the lifeboats were kept. It would have been absurd for passengers to enter the ship from an outside deck on a frigid night. And, even invited, Jack could not have joined Rose for dinner in first class: Third- and second-class passengers were strictly segregated.

MYTHS AND MYSTERIES

YOU CAN CALL THESE STORIES MARITIME (NOT URBAN) LEGENDS.

↥ Eva Hart (at center with parents above) never forgot the tragedy. "The worst thing I can remember are the screams," she said.

Over the years, it has become difficult to separate credible accounts about the *Titanic* from the fanciful tales that have arisen around it. Some of these stories are ordinary enough, but others are the sorts of tales that are told around campfires. Do you believe in psychics, ghosts, mystery dogs and ancient curses? Read on.

THE PSYCHIC PREMONITIONS

Many alleged premonitions of the *Titanic* disaster have been reported over time. One involves first-class passenger Helen Bishop, who claimed that an Egyptian fortune teller had predicted that she would survive a shipwreck, live through an earthquake and die in a car acci-

dent. Just after the sinking, Bishop and her husband were vacationing in California when an earthquake hit; they both survived. One year later, Bishop fractured her skull in a car accident, which led to mental disorders and epileptic fits. She died three years later. Yet another psychic supposedly told first-class passenger Edith Corse Evans to "beware of

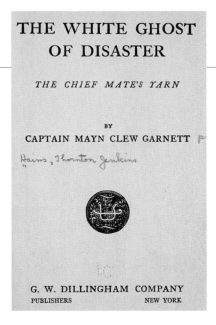

THE WHITE GHOST
OF DISASTER

THE CHIEF MATE'S YARN

BY
CAPTAIN MAYN CLEW GARNETT

Hains, Thornton Jenkins

G. W. DILLINGHAM COMPANY
PUBLISHERS   NEW YORK

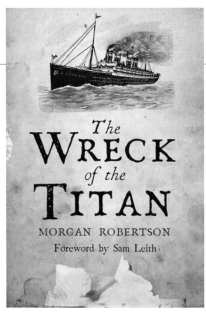

The WRECK *of the* TITAN

MORGAN ROBERTSON

Foreword by Sam Leith

→ Two of the stories that seemed to foreshadow the *Titanic* disaster (at right); William Thomas Stead (below), the muckraking journalist who ironically died on board, who wrote a few of his own.

water," a story she relayed to fellow passenger Archibald Gracie on the night of the sinking.

Second-class passenger Esther Hart's premonition of the accident stemmed from her belief that the "unsinkable" ship was "flying in the face of God." In fact, she became so alarmed that she started sleeping during the day so that she could stay vigilant at night. Awake when the ship hit the iceberg, she quickly roused her husband, Benjamin, and their young daughter, Eva, 7. Esther's prompt response may be the reason that both she and her daughter survived. (Benjamin went down with the ship.)

Chief officer Henry Wilde was originally scheduled to sail on the *Olympic*, the *Titanic*'s sister ship. When he was transferred to the *Titanic*, he wrote to his sister from Queenstown, Ireland: "I still don't like this ship," he wrote. "I have a queer feeling about it." That letter, however, has never been found.

THE FICTIONAL PREDICTIONS

In the late 1800s, first-class passenger William Thomas Stead, a journalist who died in the sinking, published two stories: "How the Mail Steamer Went Down in Mid-Atlantic, by a Survivor," about two

← A mummy's curse is said to have doomed the ship.

ships that collide, leaving passengers without enough lifeboats, and "From the Old World to the New," about a White Star Line vessel that rescues survivors of a liner that collided with an iceberg.

In 1898, Morgan Robertson published *The Wreck of the Titan,* an eerily prescient novel about the *Titan,* a British ship that is supposedly unsinkable, doesn't carry sufficient lifeboats and sinks after hitting an iceberg in the Atlantic. The novel's first line: "She was the largest craft afloat and the greatest of the works of men."

One month before the disaster, Nobel Prize–winning author Gerhart Hauptmann published *Atlantis,* a novel about a romance on a doomed ocean liner. And at the time of the sinking, an issue of *The Popular Magazine* featured a short story called "The White Ghost of Disaster," about a liner that collides with an iceberg in the Atlantic.

THE CURSES

Some believe the *Titanic* was doomed because the White Star Line didn't christen its vessels. Or was it a mummy? "Beautiful but Malignant Priestess Is Said to Resent Touching Her Coffin Lid," read the headline in the April 7, 1923, edition of *The New York Times.* The tale concerned an Egyptian mummy that supposedly put a curse on anyone who touched her sarcophagus. The story that it was on board the *Titanic* seemingly originated with Stead, who told wild tales at dinner on the night the ship sank. The mummy was later said to have gone down with the ocean liner—an impossibility, since it was then on display in the British Museum, where it remains to this day.

THE MYSTERY DOG

A large black Newfoundland dog named Rigel was supposedly responsible for saving many lives—a legend that began with an article published in *The New York Herald* shortly after the disaster. The story claimed that the dog, which allegedly belonged to

A LIFESAVING DOG? *There's no evidence any Newfoundlands were on board the* Titanic.

↑ Built just four years before the *Titanic* sank, New York City's Jane Hotel was designed for sailors. To this day, it features nautical themes and cabinlike rooms.

"WE HAD A SINGLE CHAP LIVING IN THERE AND HE RANG UP ONE DAY CONVINCED HE HAD SEEN THE GHOST OF THE CAPTAIN.... HE SAW HIM DRIFT ACROSS THE ROOM."

- Neil Bonner -

CONTEMPORARY OWNER OF THE *TITANIC* CAPTAIN'S FORMER HOME

first officer William Murdoch, helped save passengers. "For three hours he swam in the icy water where the *Titanic* went down, evidently looking for his master, and was instrumental in guiding the boatload of survivors to the gangway of the *Carpathia*," the article read. Sure, it makes for a great story...but alas, there is no evidence that Rigel ever existed.

THE GHOSTS OF THE *TITANIC*

In 1936, London ham-radio operator Gordon Cosgrave claimed to have received ghost messages from the *Titanic* and the *Carpathia*. Others have reported seeing a spectral ship in the area of the disaster and hearing distress calls, screaming and orchestral music. A couple who lived in the house where the *Titanic*'s captain, Edward Smith, was born claimed that they repeatedly saw his ghost and felt an icy chill in their bedroom. Another story alleges that Leonard Bishop, the second officer of the SS *Winterhaven*, gave a tour of his ship to a strange man in 1977. Years later, when Bishop saw Smith's picture, he recognized him as that man. A lady in black has reportedly been seen walking down the replica of the Grand Staircase at the *Titanic* exhibition in the Luxor Las Vegas, while guests at New York City's Jane Hotel—where survivors were temporarily housed after they arrived in New York—claim to have seen ghosts, felt cold spots and heard disembodied sobbing. ✳

SPIRITS ON THE STRIP
"When you're closing this place up...you hear stuff," said an employee at the Las Vegas exhibition.

THE DAILY MIRROR

SATURDAY, APRIL 20, 1912

HYMN PLAYED WHILE

A TRAGIC TUNE?
What was the final song the musicians played as the ship sank? Historians remain unsure.

THE TITANIC SANK

TRUE OR FALSE?

WHEN IT COMES TO THE MOST MYTHOLOGIZED
SHIP IN HISTORY, IT CAN BE HARD TO SEPARATE
FACT FROM FICTION—BUT HERE'S A START.

The **Titanic** *was advertised as "unsinkable."*

❌ FALSE

The most common misconception about the *Titanic* seems to have originated with a story in *Shipbuilder* magazine, which called the ship "practically unsinkable." Although White Star Line officials didn't contradict the claim, they never actively advertised the ship as such. "It's a retrospective myth, and it makes a better story," according to Richard Howells, PhD, professor of cultural sociology at King's College London. "If a man in his pride builds an unsinkable ship, like Prometheus stealing the fire from the gods...it makes perfect mythical sense that God would be so angry at such an affront that he would sink the ship on its maiden outing."

There was, however, overwhelming confidence in the *Titanic*'s seaworthiness, which is part of the reason why it set sail with so few lifeboats. At the start of the new century, ships were becoming so sophisticated and supposedly safe that officials believed they could serve as their own lifeboats. That notion was upended—along with so much else—when the *Titanic* sank.

➥ In *Titanic*, Rose (played by Kate Winslet, shown here with Leonardo DiCaprio as Jack) was not based on a real person, though some of her characteristics were "borrowed" from actual passenger Rose DeWitt Bukater.

Jack and Rose in James Cameron's movie Titanic were based on real people.

☒ FALSE

However, there were many other characters in the film who were inspired by historical figures, including Molly Brown (Kathy Bates), John Jacob Astor IV (Eric Braeden), Benjamin Guggenheim (Michael Ensign), Lady Duff-Gordon (Rosalind Ayres), and the Countess of Rothes (Rochelle Rose). (For more on the movie, see page 148.)

The Titanic had a cat.

☑ TRUE

Her name was Jenny, and she gave birth to a litter of kittens when the ship was docked at Southampton. According to survivor Violet Jessop, a stewardess on the ship, they lived in one of the galleys. The ship also carried several roosters and hens, which had belonged to passenger Ella Holmes White, who had bought them in France, as well as 12 dogs. The dogs were freed from the ship's kennel before it sank, but all the animals perished except for three small dogs, which their owners carried into the lifeboats.

←Two Pomeranians and a Pekingese were the only animals that survived.

The ship was going too fast.

☑ TRUE

Many passengers had noticed the ship's increasing speed—particularly on the night of the tragedy. "Toward evening the report, which I heard, was spread that wireless messages from passing steamers had been received advising the officers of our ship of the presence of icebergs and ice floes," first-class passenger Archibald Gracie later wrote. "The increasing cold and the necessity of being more warmly clad when appearing on deck were outward and visible signs in corroboration of these warnings. But despite them all, no diminution of speed was indicated and the engines kept up their steady running."

It has been alleged that J. Bruce Ismay, chairman of the White Star Line and a passenger on the ship, encouraged Captain Smith to increase the speed because he wanted to arrive at its New York destination early as a demonstration of the *Titanic*'s immense power. More likely, Smith thought that it was safer to speed through regions of ice: The faster you went, he reasoned, the sooner you would put the danger behind you. "Speed makes for safety under practically all conditions except for that of fog," Smith had once said.

The captain was drunk.

☒ FALSE

On the night of the tragedy, Captain Smith attended a dinner party in his honor, but witnesses later claimed that he refused to drink, since it was forbidden while on duty. One fellow diner said that the captain did take a sip of port, but this would have had no effect on his subsequent actions—or lack thereof.

In 2012, a previously unknown letter surfaced, alleging that the captain had, in fact, been drinking that night. Written by second-class passenger Emily Richards to her mother-in-law, it read, in part: "The Captain was down in the saloon drinking and gave charge to some-one else to stare [sic] the ship…. It was the Captan [sic] fault." Since no one else has ever made the same accusation, it is likely that Richards' claim was false.

The band played "Nearer, My God, to Thee" as the ship sank.

❓ UNDETERMINED

Although it's true that the musicians played to the bitter end, their last song remains a matter of debate. Wireless operator Harold Bride said that they played "Autumn," claiming that "Nearer, My God, to Thee" would have been a "tactless warning of immediate death to us all, and one likely to create panic."

Other survivors alleged that the band did indeed play "Nearer, My God, to Thee," although the story is further complicated by the fact that there are several versions of the hymn—and no one seems to know which one was played. The musicians' courage, however, has never been disputed. One survivor remembered seeing bandleader Wallace Hartley clinging to the grand staircase as the ship went down, saying to his fellow musicians, "Gentlemen, I bid you farewell."

Third-class passengers were prevented from reaching the lifeboats.

☒ FALSE

In James Cameron's *Titanic*, steerage passengers are literally locked in the bowels of the flooding ship—a particularly vivid scene that nevertheless has no basis in history. "No evidence has been given…that any attempt was made to keep back the third-class passengers," said lawyer W.D. Harbinson, who testified on their behalf before the British Inquiry Board's 1912 investigation into the disaster.

It is true that gates prevented the third-class passengers from entering the first- and second-class areas, since mixing classes was strictly forbidden by U.S. Immigration laws. Many third-class passengers were immigrants from far-flung places, and it was feared that they might spread disease. Although the gates did not prevent third-class passengers from reaching the boat deck, they did force them to travel through a labyrinth of corridors—a more complicated and time-consuming journey than people in first and second class had to make.

The men who escaped on lifeboats were cowards.

❓ NOT NECESSARILY

Although it's hard to fathom now, the magnitude of the disaster was not immediately apparent to passengers at the time. The *Titanic*'s captain had not given an "abandon ship" command, for one thing, and the crew downplayed the situation to avoid creating panic. Many passengers felt that the ship would eventually be repaired and that climbing into the lifeboats would merely expose them

↑ James Cameron's *Titanic* largely depicts the men who escaped on the lifeboats as villains. Sure, some of them were, but it wasn't quite that simple.

to the cold. Others believed that, even if the ship sank, they would be safer aboard than in the frigid water.

As a result, there was little initial demand for the lifeboats, some of which were launched well under capacity. The fact that many women refused to board them led a handful of men to take their places. If they hadn't, some of the vessels would have been even emptier than they already were.

Many male survivors—particularly J. Bruce Ismay—spent the rest of their lives wrestling with guilt, shame and widespread accusations of cowardice. Especially among the British, considerable emphasis was placed on the proverbial stiff upper lip and a stoic acceptance of fate. Newspaper accounts of the disaster celebrated the quiet heroism of the men who went down with the ship and condemned those who lived. ✳

IN THE DEPTHS
Some operators are providing an up-close view of shipwrecks like the Titanic.

EXPERIENCE THE *TITANIC*

EVEN THOUGH THE SHIP HAS BEEN UNDERWATER FOR OVER A CENTURY, MUSEUMS, TOURS AND EVEN VIDEO GAMES PROVIDE EXCITING WAYS TO ENGAGE WITH THE LEGENDARY VESSEL.

TITANIC II

When launched in 1912, the *Titanic* was first viewed as a triumph of engineering, a massive shrine to human ingenuity. But once tragedy took place, it became the opposite: an allegory of the pitfalls of hubris. No ship, it turns out, is truly unsinkable. Such a terrible end seemed to beg for a second attempt, a chance to do it the right way. But who would dare take on a project with that much psychological baggage?

Enter Clive Palmer, an enigmatic Australian billionaire and the man behind *Titanic II*. In 2012, Palmer announced the formation of Blue Star Line—named for *Titanic* company White Star Line—and a *Titanic II* launch for 2016. After years of delays, Palmer returned in 2018 to declare that the project was back on, and that the ship would launch from Dubai in 2022.

"The ship will follow the original journey, carrying passengers from Southampton to New York, but she will also circumnavigate the globe, inspiring and enchanting people while attracting unrivaled attention, intrigue and mystery in every port she visits," said Palmer.

Naturally, the *Titanic II* will have substantial technological and safety

→ The *Titanic II* will mirror the original ship in many ways, with its vintage decor and luxury-minded details, but with a few modern updates (including electronic navigation and enough lifeboats for all).

upgrades compared to its forebear from a century ago. The new ship will have a welded hull rather than a riveted one, digital navigation systems and will run on diesel fuel instead of coal. (The four smokestacks remain part of the design anyway.) And crucially, the new boat will have modern lifeboats—and enough of them for everyone on board.

But modern amenities aside, the project is an effort to recreate the original *Titanic* to a T, from the matching menu design to the identical sweeping grand staircase.

"Blue Star Line will create an authentic *Titanic* experience, providing passengers with a ship that has the same interiors and cabin layout as the original vessel," Palmer said.

Titanic fans seeking luxurious cocktail parties at sea and those inclined to take a more economical vacation should both find a suitable trip on *Titanic II*. Just like the original, it will sell first-, second-, and third-class tickets.

OCEANGATE EXPEDITIONS

As a general rule, the world's most interesting landmarks are fairly easy to visit. With a few days of vacation and a plane ticket, anyone can visit the Eiffel Tower in Paris, the Colosseum in Rome or the Great Wall of China. The *Titanic*, of course, is a notable exception, thanks to its deep-sea locale.

But for the die-hard enthusiasts, there is at least one way to get close to the buried ship. In 2021, OceanGate

↑ "Mission specialists" (aka paying customers) aren't just tourists on board OceanGate Expeditions' *Titanic* exploration.

Expeditions is organizing dives to visit the ship's remaining wreckage that are open to the (paying) public.

"More people have climbed Everest than have seen the *Titanic*," says OceanGate head Stockton Rush. "If you want to do something truly unique that also advances man's knowledge, then underwater is where you've got to do it."

The once-in-a-lifetime experience will require a once-in-a-lifetime investment: to help underwrite the trip, participants must contribute $125,000 for a 10- to 14-day voyage. But this is no luxury vacation. It's an opportunity to truly participate in a meaningful underwater study of a vessel that disintegrates further with each passing year.

"If this were just another money-losing wealthy person's activity, I don't see how it scales," Rush says. "We don't take passengers, we don't

↑ OceanGate Expeditions plans to conduct annual scientific and technological surveys of the wreck, including videos and photos of the site and its surrounding flora and fauna.

On the support ship, tasks include dive planning, communications and tracking, and dive image review. Those who board the submersible *Titan* will be charged with handling navigation, sonar operation, laser scanning and photography. Each mission specialist will make one dive in the submarine.

With the rate at which the ship is breaking down as it lies at the bottom of the ocean, these mission specialists may be some of the last people to view the *Titanic* in a recognizable state. If all goes according to plan, they may also be the first underwater visitors to see certain elements of the ship.

"The amount of time we are going to spend out will allow us to find things that others have missed," says Rush.

VIRTUAL REALITY

Don't have tens of thousands of dollars on hand to join an expedition? No problem. With the right equipment, you can dive to the wreckage on your own. You can even swim into the ship, exploring the rooms as they appeared during the first *Titanic* recovery expeditions in the late '80s—all from the comfort of your living room.

At least, that's the promise of Titanic VR, an educational virtual reality video game from Immersive VR Education. Available on virtual reality gaming platforms such as Oculus and PlayStation VR, the game puts players in charge of their own recovery mission in the deep blue waters.

do trips, we don't do rides. We're doing an expedition," he adds. "Everyone will have an active role. I need people who understand that this is a mission with a scientific purpose."

With that in mind, guest members of the crew will receive the title of mission specialist. And indeed each specialist's duties will be significant, chosen based on the individual's skills and interests. There are jobs to be done both aboard a support ship and on *Titan*, the only submarine of its (small) size capable of traveling as deep as the *Titanic*'s resting spot at about 12,500 feet below the surface.

"We decided to make our digital *Titanic* shipwreck based on information and surveys from 1986–1987, when the wreck was better preserved and easier to explore," says Immersive VR Education CEO David Whelan. "Our digital exterior of the wreck from this period is quite accurate. For the interior of the shipwreck, we had to mix information from later dives and, in some cases, make an educated call on the state of preservation of some of the bedrooms that haven't been explored before. We wanted to open up as much of the ship as possible, allowing people to freely explore. Our interpretation of areas that no [remotely operated underwater vehicle] has been before will be available to view inside Titanic VR."

But the dive is just one of two components of Titanic VR's gameplay. The other takes you back to 1912 and places you on board to witness *Titanic*'s vastness, splendor and, ultimately, its demise. Depicting real passengers and crew members, Titanic VR includes the most real-life animated characters of any VR experience ever made.

"We wanted to create an accurate portrayal of events, so it is not only educational, but also emotional and very engaging," Whelan says. "To achieve that we used motion capture, face-scanning technology and professional voice actors to immerse users in the story and to enable them to relate to the people involved."

So if you've ever dreamed of being on the *Titanic*—or in the movie *Titanic*—virtual reality is as close as it gets.

TITANIC MUSEUMS

With collections of unique artifacts and exhibits curated by experts, museums present unparalleled opportunities to learn about the history and journey of the *Titanic*.

Few experiences capture the heart and soul of the tragic tale like Titanic Belfast, at the former Harland & Wolff shipyard where the vessel was built from 1909 to 1911. Visitors can set foot on the world's last remaining White Star Line ship, SS *Nomadic*, which was built to deliver first- and second-class passengers to the *Titanic* from the shore. Artifacts on site include letters from passengers, ornate White Star china, and a first-class luncheon menu from the ship's final day afloat. (Passengers were served mutton chops.) To get around museum grounds, ride on

⬇ With Titanic VR, you can witness the sinking of the ship from the perspective of a passenger or plunge into the watery depths to explore the wreckage at the bottom of the North Atlantic.

⇡ Visitors to the SeaCity Museum in Southampton, England, can get an up-close look at some of the officers and crew members who set off on the *Titanic*, as well as interactive experiences on a model replica ship.

the Wee Tram—a tram car modeled after those that *Titanic* builders took to and from the shipyard.

In 1987, John Joslyn led a $6 million expedition to the *Titanic* wreckage in the Atlantic Ocean. Years later, the historian sought to share his love of the ship by opening two Titanic Museum Attractions—one in Branson, Missouri, and one in Pigeon Forge, Tennessee. "I want to share as closely as possible with guests what *Titanic*'s actual passengers and crew experienced aboard ship," Joslyn writes. "Visitors can touch finely carved wooden inlays, grasp the wheel on the captain's bridge, tap out messages on the ship's wireless, feel an iceberg's chill, stroll decks and galleries and listen to stories told by real survivors."

As the site of the *Titanic*'s departure—and former home to much of its crew—no city identifies more closely with the ship than Southampton, England. So it's fitting that the city is home to one of *Titanic*'s foremost attractions in SeaCity Museum. Opened in 2012 during the *Titanic* centennial remembrance, the museum offers guests the opportunity to explore replicas of the ship and the courtroom where the British inquiry into the disaster took place. An interactive virtual ship lets them take the wheel of the ship or stoke its engine to propel it forward. And after a long day of learning and exploring, visitors can enjoy a beer from nearby Titanic Brewery. *

IN MEMORIAM

ALL AROUND THE WORLD, MONUMENTS TO VICTIMS
OF THE TITANIC SHIPWRECK REMIND US OF
WHAT WAS LOST IN APRIL 1912.

TITANIC ENGINEERS' MEMORIAL AND TITANIC MUSICIANS' MEMORIAL

Southampton, England

As 539 of the lives lost in the sinking of the *Titanic* belonged to residents of Southampton, no locale was hit harder by the tragedy. Made of copper and bronze, this memorial depicts Nike, the Greek goddess of victory. It was unveiled to a crowd of 100,000 on April 22, 1914, just over two years after the tragedy.

Across the street is the Musicians' Memorial, which pays tribute to the band members aboard the *Titanic*. The original memorial was destroyed in a World War II bombing, but a replica was built and installed in 1990.

IN MEMORY
OF THE
HEROIC MUSICIANS
OF THE S.S "TITANIC"
LOST ON HER MAIDEN VOYAGE FROM SOUTHAMPTON TO NEW YORK
APRIL 15th 1912

C. KRINS.   W. HARTLEY   R. BRICOUX

W. T. BRAILEY   J. WOODWARD

J. F. CLARKE   J. L. HUME

P. C. TAYLOR
THEY DIED AT THEIR POSTS LIKE MEN
ERECTED BY THE MEMBERS   UNVEILED BY
AND FRIENDS   HIS WORSHIP THE MAYOR
OF THE AMALGAMATED MUSICIANS
UNION   COUNCILLOR H BOWYER R.N.R
SOUTHAMPTON BRANCH   APRIL 16 1913

TITANIC MEMORIAL

Belfast, Ireland

The city where the *Titanic* was
built, Belfast lost 22 of its own men
in the disaster. This memorial was
originally dedicated in 1920, and in
2012—exactly a century after the
shipwreck—a garden was added
to the site. While most *Titanic*
memorials commemorate specific
groups of people who were aboard
the boat, the Belfast memorial
is dedicated to all the victims—
passengers and crew alike—listing
the names of 1,512 lost souls.

TITANIC MEMORIAL BANDSTAND

Ballarat, Victoria, Australia

One of the more distinctive-
looking *Titanic* memorials, the
Bandstand in Victoria is one of
several worldwide that honors the
musicians who died in the disaster.
Members of the Victoria Band
Association were moved by the
tragedy, which compelled them to
raise funds for the memorial. When
it was unveiled in 1915, Australian
musicians traveled from far and
wide to pay their respects.

PAYING HOMAGE
The memorial is dedicated to the men of the Titanic*, who made up about 75% of the victims.*

TITANIC MEMORIAL
Washington, D.C.

In the near aftermath of the tragedy, the Women's Titanic Memorial Committee was formed to raise money for a memorial. It held a women-only design competition, which was won by sculptor Gertrude Vanderbilt Whitney. Her work was displayed in Rock Creek Park when first unveiled in 1931. In 1968, it was moved to its current location in Washington Channel Park.

TITANIC MEMORIAL LIGHTHOUSE
New York City

Originally located along the East River when constructed in 1913, this memorial was built partly at the behest of famous *Titanic* passenger Margaret Brown, aka "The Unsinkable Molly Brown." Up until 1967, the lighthouse would signal the timing of noon to ships offshore to help them calibrate their chronometers. In 1976, it was moved to the South Street Seaport Museum on Fulton Street.

ST. PETER THE APOSTLE ROMAN CATHOLIC CHURCH
Libertytown, Maryland

The Rev. Joseph Kavanaugh was renovating his church's garden when he first learned of the *Titanic* news, and immediately acted to commemorate the victims. He installed an honorary plaque on April 19, 1912, only four days after the wreck. It is widely believed to be the first *Titanic* memorial ever installed. The plaque was rededicated on April 15, 2012, the centennial anniversary of the sinking.

THE DISASTER BY THE NUMBERS

1 MILE
THE LIKELY ORIGINAL LENGTH OF THE *TITANIC* ICEBERG

200
MILLIONS OF DOLLARS JAMES CAMERON'S *TITANIC* COST TO MAKE

3,000,000
NUMBER OF RIVETS USED IN THE SHIP'S HULL

2
NUMBER OF WORKERS KILLED DURING THE BUILDING OF THE SHIP

37 SECONDS
THE AMOUNT OF TIME FROM THE FIRST SIGHTING OF THE ICEBERG TO THE IMPACT

The approximate number of light bulbs on the ship

10,000

3
THE NUMBER OF DOGS (OUT OF 12 ON BOARD) THAT SURVIVED THE SINKING

$7.5M

HOW MUCH THE *TITANIC* COST TO BUILD

THE NUMBER OF HORSES NEEDED TO CARRY THE SHIP'S MAIN ANCHOR

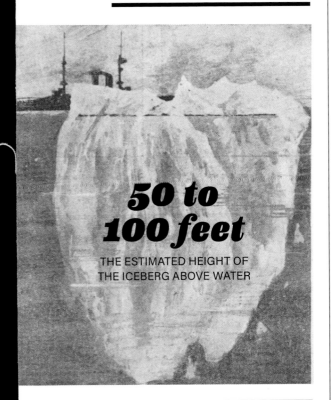

50 to 100 feet

THE ESTIMATED HEIGHT OF THE ICEBERG ABOVE WATER

2 WEEKS

THE TIME THE FATAL ICEBERG LIKELY LASTED AFTER THE COLLISION

100%

CHILDREN SAVED FROM SECOND CLASS

825

Tons of coal used on the ship per day

19

THE NUMBER OF ICEBERGS THAT SURVIVOR CHARLES DAHL LATER CLAIMED HE HAD SEEN FROM LIFEBOAT NO. 15

CENTENNIAL BOOKS

An Imprint of
Centennial Media, LLC
40 Worth St., 10th Floor
New York, NY 10013, U.S.A.

CENTENNIAL BOOKS is a trademark of Centennial Media, LLC

ISBN 978-1-951274-83-2

Distributed by
Simon & Schuster, Inc.
1230 Avenue of the Americas
New York, NY 10020, U.S.A.

For information about custom editions, special sales and premium and corporate purchases,
please contact Centennial Media at contact@centennialmedia.com.

Manufactured in Singapore

© 2021 by Centennial Media, LLC

10 9 8 7 6 5 4 3 2 1